THE
New Guideposts
Christmas Treasury

THE
New Guideposts
Christmas Treasury

Compiled by the editors
of *Guideposts*®

AUGSBURG ◆ MINNEAPOLIS

ACKNOWLEDGMENTS

Every attempt has been made to credit the sources of copyrighted material used in this book. If any such acknowledgment has been inadvertently omitted or miscredited, receipt of such information would be appreciated.

"The Miracle of Christmas," by Helen Steiner Rice is used by permission of the Helen Steiner Rice Foundation.

"A Gift of the Heart," by Norman Vincent Peace is reprinted with permission from the January 1968 Reader's Digest. Copyright 1967 by The Reader's Digest Assn., Inc.

"Christmas Is Always," by Dale Evans Rogers is reprinted from *Christmas Is Always*. Copyright 1958 by Fleming H. Revell Co.

"As a Little Child," from *Miss Humpety Comes to Tea* by Grace Noll Crowell. Copyright, 1927, 1938 by Harper & Row, Publishers, Inc. Copyright, 1957, 1966 by Grace Noll Crowell. Reprinted by permission of Harper & Row, Publishers, Inc.

"My Most Memorable Christmas," by Catherine Marshall is adapted from *Family Weekly*. It is reprinted from Guideposts Magazine, Copyright © 1965 by Guideposts Associates, Inc., Carmel, New York 10512.

"The Gift That Kept Giving," by Marion Bond West; and "A Christmas Reminder," by Ruth A. Ritchie are reprinted from *The Guideposts Family Christmas Book*. Copyright © 1980 by Guideposts Associates, Inc., Carmel, New York 10512.

"My Christmas Prayer," by Rosalyn Hart Finch; "A Straw-Filled Christmas Tradition," by Lynne Laukhuf; and "The Message from the Manger," by June Masters Bacher are reprinted from *The Gifts of Christmas*, Copyright © 1981 by Guideposts Associates, Inc., Carmel, New York 10512.

"This Day," by Rosalyn Hart Finch and "A Christmas List" by Marilyn Morgan Helleberg are reprinted from *The Treasures of Christmas*. Copyright © 1982 by Guideposts Associates, Inc., Carmel, New York 10512.

"A Christmas Garden," by Van Varner and "The Christmas I Remember Best," by Rheuama West are reprinted from *Daily Guideposts, 1980*. Copyright © 1979 by Guideposts Associates, Inc., Carmel, New York 10512.

"Mary's Meditations," by Sue Monk Kidd are reprinted from *Daily Guideposts, 1983*. Copyright © 1982 by Guideposts Associates, Inc., Carmel, New York 10512.

"Meet Me in the City," by Van Varner is reprinted from *Daily Guideposts, 1985*. Copyright © 1984 by Guideposts Associates, Inc., Carmel, New York 10512.

Excerpt from *I've Got to Talk to Somebody, God* by Marjorie Holmes, copyright © 1968 by Marjorie Holmes Mighell. Used by permission of Doubleday, a division of Bantam, Doubleday, Dell Publishing Group, Inc.

Designed by Lorraine Mullaney

Library of Congress Catalog Card No. 89-45532
International Standard Book No. 0-8066-2416-7

THE New Guideposts Christmas Treasury

The Warmth of Christmas in the Family

The Wonder of Christmas and Children

The Joy of Christmas Memories

The First Christmas

The Light of Christmas Love

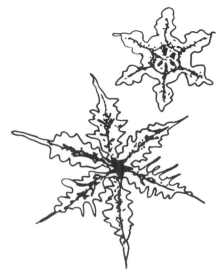

The Happiness of Christmas Sharing

The Blessings of Christmas Giving

The
Miracles
of Christmas

Epilogue:
A Lasting
Christmas

Introduction

Perhaps no writings have touched our hearts more than the narratives of Christmas. Since childhood we have known and cherished the old classic stories of the Holy Season. Every year we like to read them over again, even though we know them well. Their charm never fades; their truth abides in all generations.

All lovers of good books try to build a home library consisting of truly great works to inspire and help all members of the family. Perhaps a family becomes what it reads. And families are entitled to the best.

That's the reason we at Guideposts always seek to provide the best in Christian literature for our readers. In the past we have made available many fine volumes. Now here is another book that will be a prized possession in every home library. *The New Guideposts Christmas Treasury* is the most comprehensive collection of Christmas stories we have ever seen. It includes choice narratives based on the Nativity, beloved classic stories of Christmas, and newer stories, many of which may themselves become classics.

For ready use, the *Treasury* is divided into nine sections, plus an Epilogue. The inspirational pieces, poems, and moving stories of the first section, "The Presence of Christmas in the Heart," show that Christmas is a time of deep inner feeling that lifts one to high levels of joy.

The second section, "The Warmth of Christmas in the Family," will remind every reader of their own family experiences of love and happiness over the years. These selections might very well be read aloud to your family around the Christmas fireplace.

The very title of section three, "The Wonder of Christmas and Children," produces a sense of expectation and excitement. Christmas is especially for children, whatever their age, from infancy to ninety. The latter may wistfully quote from Elizabeth Akers Allen's poem "Rock Me to Sleep":

> Backward, turn backward, O Time, in your flight,
> Make me a child again just for tonight!

You see, Christmas works a strange and marvelous alchemy in minds that are tired and hearts that are heavy, by investing even older people with the eternal youthfulness of faith. Always the sense of wonder is renewed at Christmastime.

So this wonderful new *Christmas Treasury* goes on in more fascinating sections: "The Joy of Christmas Memories," "The First Christmas," "The Light of Christmas Love," "The Happiness of Christmas Sharing," and "The Blessings of Christmas Giving." This last-named section contains one of our own favorite Christmas stories, that of Ursula from Switzerland who lived with us for several years.

The New Guideposts Christmas Treasury closes with a section on "The Miracles of Christmas," six heartwarming stories that tell us once again that Christmas is a time for the strange and wonderful works of God.

The last note of the book is sounded by the Epilogue which reminds us of what the world would be if we were to hold the Christmas spirit in our hearts all year long. What God wants to make of the world He told us on that star-studded night so long ago when He laid a Baby on the doorstep of the world. He said that we should love one another.

—*Norman Vincent Peale*
—*Ruth Stafford Peale*

The presence of Christmas in the heart

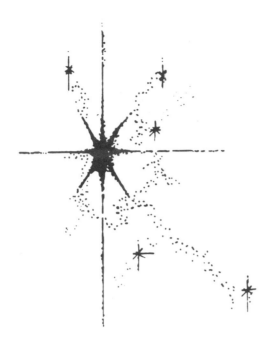

My Christmas Prayer

Dearest God, please never let me
Crowd my life full to the brim,
So like the keeper of Bethlehem's inn,
I find I have no room for Him.

Instead, let my heart's door be ever open,
Ready to welcome the newborn King,
Let me offer the best I have,
To Him who gives me everything.

—Rosalyn Hart Finch

The Underground Angels

On Christmas Eve, after getting off my typing job at noon, I stood dejectedly in the crowd waiting for the subway train. I had worked by myself all morning, since all my fellow workers had been given the day off. Many people around me were talking happily about their trips home to their families. Some had little children with them. I had no home—just a rented room—no plans, no husband and no children, although I was getting well into my thirties.

Suddenly, I heard the crystal notes of two flutes interweaving. Down the platform were two young girls, playing Christmas carols. In their serene young beauty, they looked like angels in disguise.

I added my quarter to the pile of change in their open flute cases. The train came and went, but I lingered, fascinated by the people who came forward to drop coins, even bills. Most were shabbily dressed, but their faces seemed alight with happiness. These were the poor, the people Christ had greatly loved. On that cold, noisy subway platform they were joined, without knowing one another, in the great Christmas Feast of Love that I had lost sight of in my self-pity.

Finally, I heard the girls play "O Little Town of Bethlehem" and I found myself remembering words that I had not sung since my childhood. "O Holy Child of Bethlehem, descend to us, we pray. Cast out our sin and enter in; be born in us today." And suddenly, there in this bleak subway station, everything was changed. Of course I had a Christmas feast to go to! The Lord's Supper at church that evening. Of course I had a home! "For where two or three are gathered together in my name, there am I in the midst of them."* Of course I had a child! The Holy Child could be born in me every day as I sought to love Him above and beyond the hope for a worldly marriage and children.

I took the next train, feeling warm and contented. I knew that those two young strangers had given me a magnificent Christmas gift. They had put Christ back where He belonged—in Christmas and in my heart.

—*Margaret B. Waage*

*Matthew 18:20.

A Straw-Filled Christmas Tradition

It all began a few years ago. It was several weeks before Christmas, and our family was busy preparing for the holiday. Excitement was everywhere. Our two children, Adam, aged three, and Shannon, aged eight, delighted in baking and frosting the Christmas cookies; I was running around doing errands and Christmas shopping; and my husband, Larry, was out searching for the perfect tree. The traditional wreath had gone up on the front door, and inside the house, candles, holly and a garland completed the festive look.

But one afternoon, following a long day of baking and gift-wrapping, I walked into the living room, sank my weary body into the sofa and propped my tired feet on the coffee table. The excitement of the holiday had turned to exhaustion and the joy of the season was fading. *Where in all of these preparations,* I wondered, *is the message that Christ has come into the world?* Our family, it seemed to me, was so busy *preparing* for Christmas that perhaps we'd lost sight of its true meaning.

That evening I told Larry about my concern. "How *can* we put Christ into our Christmas?" I asked him. He seemed to agree with me that materialism had taken hold in our house and we ought to get our attention back to the spiritual—Christ's coming.

No, we didn't decree an end to our Christmas festivities, but we did add a preparation that was to become meaningful to all of us. We took our manger scene and placed it in a prominent place in the dining room. As usual, the children carefully unpacked the plaster of paris figures that had been saved from my husband's childhood, and placed them around the manger.

However, we left the infant crib empty. Next to the manger we placed a small bowl filled with pieces of straw. Since all children understand that babies need a soft, comfortable bed in which to lie, we explained that we had to get ready for the Baby Jesus to come and that we would fill His crib with bits of straw.

Then we told them about the most important part of this new family tradition. "Giving gifts at Christmas is a message of love," Larry explained. "You can give gifts to the Baby Jesus, too." The children's faces lit up.

"That's right," I picked up. "We won't give Him presents wrapped in ribbons and bows, but we can do kind and loving things for others, in His name. And each and every time we do a kindness for someone else, we will put a piece of straw in the empty crib. By Christmas we'll have our special gift for the Baby Jesus." The little ones nodded and beamed with excitement. They were eager to begin.

During those weeks before Christmas a special anticipation was added to our home. Small deeds of kindness were secretly performed and the bed was slowly filling . . .

One afternoon when I came home, the dirty breakfast dishes had been washed and cleared from the dishwasher. After a snow-filled day of sledding, Adam (with a little help from his dad) had secretly put away Shannon's sled for the night. A call from Nana told us of the special hand-drawn pictures the children had sent in the Christmas mail. And one morning, we awoke to find two round, shining faces awaiting us with "breakfast in bed"—a bowl filled with milk and a few spoonfuls of cereal.

So it went. I even discovered my son's little playmate quietly slipping into the house to put in a few bits of straw. Little surprises never ceased and the manger was looking quite comfortable with its thick bed of hay.

On Christmas morning the crib was full and Shannon carefully placed the Baby in His love-filled bed. After breakfast we gathered around the manger with a specially baked birthday cake and sang, "Happy Birthday to Jesus."

Each year we repeat this family tradition it becomes more special. And as we sing to Him on Christmas morning we remember it is His day after all and that we have prepared ourselves for His coming and have given Him many fine gifts of love.

—*Lynne Laukhuf*

How to Welcome the Christ Child

"Behold, I bring you good tidings of great joy, which shall be to all people. For unto you is born this day in the city of David a Saviour, which is Christ the Lord."*

No other news ever delivered to human beings can approach in happiness this simple statement of a birth. The Scripture says that His name shall be called Emmanuel,** which means—God with us. This is the heart of the Christmas message, that Almighty God abides with us.

What a glorious truth! He Who rolled back the curtain of the night at the dawn of creation, He Who hung the stars in spangled glory upon the skies, He Who sets the sun in motion, and the planets according to their orbits, the eternal everlasting Creator and Ruler of the ends of the earth—He, according to this story, is with us; with you and with me. This is the only wonder of the world. The greatest, finest, most intellectual men among us have discovered this truth in their personal experiences.

Why did Christ come? Have you asked yourselves this? When last did you think about it?

He came to save the world. To redeem us from our sins. And to show us how to live.

Now those of us who have come to love and serve God have learned how practical are His teachings, how never failing His help, how ever dependable His advice and directions. We use His way of life, knowing it works daily miracles—and yet we sometimes wonder why it doesn't solve everything.

Is it because we shun the first and real mission of His coming? To save us from our sins—us sinners?

The modern generation does not like to talk about sin; some even go so far as to say there is no sin. Well, what shall we call it? Is it just sophistication? As a matter of fact the word does not apply, because a man who lives a sinful life is not sophisticated, he is a fool. Sophistica-

*Luke 2:10–11.   **Matthew 1:23.

tion means to be worldly-wise, to know your way around in the world so you will not get licked by the world. But those sinful ones who call themselves sophisticated *are* licked. What is their trouble? They are doing wrong and they cannot stop it. So they try to rationalize it.

Rationalization is when the mind tells you that what you are doing is not wrong—it used to be wrong years ago, but it is not wrong anymore. Whenever you do a wrong thing your mind tries to save face. It always says to you, "Now wait a minute, what you did is not wrong at all; you are really a very fine fellow. These preachers are all out-of-date, behind the times—do not believe them, talking about sin and the like!" That is the way the mind sometimes works.

I once heard a very wise man say something that brought me up short. A university president and author of numerous books, he observed: "The smartest thing the devil ever did was to get people to believe that the devil does not exist."

We believe in God Who is a Spirit. We believe in a Universal force that is spiritual. We believe we ourselves have an imperishable spirit. Yes, we believe in the power of the spirit of good. We believe the Bible. But too many of us dismiss the power of the spirit of evil, though we see its work all about us.

The devil? Sin? Archaic, childish, old-fashioned, don't you know! And certainly not scientific.

But Christ came to our earth to save mankind from sin—to redeem us—to be our personal salvation. He gave us tools of infinite worth to build our road to Heaven.

Yes, we have a world full of conflict and hate—but God is with us. We cannot save ourselves, but in Him we put our trust.

If today—this minute—we open our hearts and embrace Him and His teachings—not only to reap abundance and joy and health and happy fulfillment, but also for the cancellation of our sins—then this is the greatest welcome we can give to the Christ Child.

—*Norman Vincent Peale*

The Search

I looked for Christmas everywhere,
Through snow-filled skies and winter's air.
I hunted in the likely places—
The festive shops, the children's faces.

I searched for Christmas day and night,
In sprigs of holly, candlelight;
In gifts gay-wrapped and friendly greeting,
Yet found it not, and time was fleeting.

And then—with such a sudden start—
I thought to search within my heart.
And there—not lost, but warm and waking—
Was Christmas, mine just for the taking!

—*Emily Templeton*

Mother's Colossal Cookie Caper

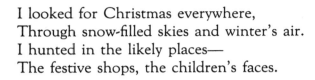

When I was a little girl, I had a friend whose Polish grandmother always set an extra place at the family table on Christmas Day. I can still remember her explaining in heavily accented English, "We should always be ready to receive the Lord into our hearts and homes. Who knows when He will come again?"

Every Christmas, without fail, her words would twinkle on into remembrance like so many bright Christmas tree lights. But it wasn't until the year of what my husband jokingly called Mother's Colossal

Christmas Cookie Caper that those words took on a dimension of meaning far greater than I had imagined.

Had Christmas not fallen on a Saturday that year, I might never have been inspired—three days before the approaching holiday—to invite fifty neighborhood families to a Sunday afternoon cookie and punch party.

My husband and three teenage boys tried to temper my enthusiasm with reason: not much time to plan . . . awfully close to Christmas . . . too late to send out invitations.

Already way ahead of them, I interrupted, "I've started inviting people by phone. So far the consensus is *super idea!* Almost everyone responded with something like, 'Sounds like a lot of fun—we'll do our best to be there.'

"Anyway, isn't Christmas a time to reach out lovingly to neighbors? Let's be spontaneous!"

What my menfolk didn't know was that hidden behind my sudden burst of spontaneity was a fantasy I had nurtured my whole married life: to give the kind of holiday party that glitters right off the pages of family magazine Christmas issues. The ingredients of these parties never varied—a beautifully decorated home, a superabundance of Christmas treats, a gracious host and hostess, soft candlelight, and a houseful of guests, their faces wreathed in smiles of joyful appreciation.

Ignoring my family's looks of dismay and pleas for caution, I raced on, "We can put some Christmas lights on the two evergreens by the front door, weave some ribbon and garlands through the stair rails, hang a mistletoe ball over the hall doorway and bank red poinsettias in the bay window." Then I added confidently, "I know we can do it if we all cooperate, if we all make it a family project."

"Well, boys," said my husband with a sigh of resignation, "it looks like your mother is really serious about having a Colossal Christmas Cookie Caper here Sunday afternoon." They all knew their fates had been sealed.

How we ever got from December 22nd to December 26th still remains a Yuletide blur of tangled evergreen roping, twice-vacuumed carpets, closets jammed with newly opened gifts, and freshly baked cookies popping out of the oven at all hours of the day and night.

By three o'clock Sunday afternoon we were ready. Our dining room table was a tantalizing mosaic of homemade Christmas cookies of almost every kind and shape imaginable. I was poised by the cranberry-red punch bowl. My husband and sons were stationed at the front door. Our springer spaniel, sporting a red velvet bow for the occasion, lay by the hearth. It was picture perfect—*almost*. All we lacked was the house full of mirthful guests!

As the minutes ticked beyond the first hour, I sensed something was amiss. Only a handful of neighbors had made their way to our front door. The party was very quiet and very small. By the end of the second hour I felt the cookie party crumbling all around me. Only a few more guests had straggled in to exchange holiday greetings. I waited and hoped for a last-minute rush that never materialized.

What could have gone wrong? Hadn't everyone sounded interested and excited on the phone about coming?

At that moment I wasn't at all ready for the explanations that would surface later: "tired children," "unexpected guests," "late arrival home," and even "sorry, we just forgot." Of course, when I had issued the invitations on the phone, I had tried to sound casual. Apparently I had overdone it.

As we were packing away plates and cups in the after-party cleanup, my husband tried to console me: "Everything looked terrific. I think the folks who did come really enjoyed themselves."

"The cookies were sensational," the youngest chimed in.

"Yeah, but what are we going to do with the zillions of cookies that are left?" asked his brother. "There's way too many even for *us* to eat."

I stared at the pyramids of lemon bars, holiday date squares, orange and spice drops, chocolate kisses and pralines—not to mention the traditional Christmas cutouts. Leftover cookies hadn't been in my plan.

"I'll just put them all here in the cupboard," I replied. "If any of you can think of something to do with them, go ahead, but don't bother me about it." I banged the cupboard door shut on my hurt and disappointment.

No one mentioned "cookies" or "party" at our house all that week. That's why I was amazed at week's end to open the cupboard and find not one cookie crumb in sight. Where had they all gone?

I personally could account for only two boxes. I had taken them right off to the nursing home. There, my sightless friend had traced the shape of each cookie I pressed into his hand, joyfully discovering angels, stars and gingerbread boys.

Over the dinner table that night the rest of the mystery was quickly solved. My husband had taken a box to a friend at work who had sprained his ankle Christmas Day. Our oldest son had given two boxes to a friend, who took them to a nearby prison where he was a volunteer. Our middle son gave a box to new people who moved into the neighborhood three days after Christmas. Our youngest son gave a box to a woman on his paper route who a short time before had lost her son and husband in a tragic accident.

I suddenly felt that more than one mystery was being solved here. Echoes from childhood: "We should always be ready to receive the Lord into our hearts and homes."

But I had given no invitation. I had set no place. My heart had been filled to overflowing with pride and vanity, all focused on a magazine-perfect party. There had been no room for our Lord there. Only after the party had I made it possible for us all to prepare Him room.

"Did you know," I asked softly, "that we gave a second Christmas party? It was a huge success. All the right people came. We even had a very special guest, an uninvited guest."

"What do you mean?" asked my husband in a puzzled tone.

"Who?" the boys chorused.

"Remember, *When you give food and drink to the least of these—the stranger, the sick, the blind, the imprisoned—you do it to Me.*"*

All eyes met over the kitchen table; there was no doubt in anyone's heart or mind Who that special guest was.

—*Deana Kohl*

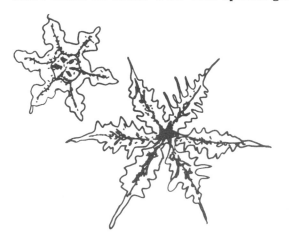

*See Matthew 25:35–40.

Christmas Is a Time for Adoration

At holiday time each year, local artists paint Christmas scenes on the store windows of our town. Not long ago my husband and I watched from the inside of our paint store as a young lady began her work. Would it be another Santa? we wondered.

First, in one corner of the window, a star was drawn. Then, in another corner, came a white lamb, and gradually, with growing pleasure, we began to see the outline of a human figure. At last our artist invited us outside to see the finished work: the first Christmas—a Madonna, the Child cradled in her lap. The painting may not have been a masterpiece, but it was so loving, so sincere, that I was moved.

The three of us crossed the street for another perspective and, as we did, a car drove up and parked down the block. A mother and her four children tumbled out and hurried merrily down the street, pointing with appreciation at the various Santas and snow scenes. When they came to our store, however, one of the children—the littlest one, a boy—lagged behind and stopped.

He stood there motionless, gazing at the Christ Child as though transfixed. Then the lad rose on his tiptoes, reached up, and in a gesture of boyish reverence, touched the Babe's tiny fingers.

"Oh!" the artist gasped. "The paint's still wet." And when we crossed over to look, there was indeed a tiny smudge on the picture's surface. The artist took out her brush to repair it, but my husband stopped her.

"Please leave it," he said. I knew what he meant. Throughout the season, that little smudge reminded us that Christmas is a time for unabashed adoration of our Savior.

—*Ruth Ikerman*

Take Hold of Love

I was working feverishly on my Christmas sermon—the hardest time in any minister's year to find something fresh to say—when the floor mother appeared at the study door. Another crisis upstairs. Christmas Eve is a difficult day for the emotionally disturbed children in our church home. Three-quarters of them go home at least overnight and the ones who remain react to the empty beds and the changed routine.

I followed her up the stairs, chafing inwardly at the repeated interruptions. This time it was Tommy. He had crawled under a bed and refused to come out. The woman pointed to one of six cots in the small dormitory. Not a hair or a toe showed beneath it, so I addressed myself to the cowboys and bucking broncos on the bedspread. I talked about the brightly lighted tree in the church vestibule next door and the packages underneath it and all the other good things waiting for him out beyond that bed.

No answer.

Still fretting at the time this was costing, I dropped to my hands and knees and lifted the spread. Two enormous blue eyes met mine. Tommy was eight, but looked like a five-year-old. It would have been no effort at all simply to pull him out. But it wasn't pulling that Tommy needed—it was trust and a sense of deciding things on his own initiative. So, crouched there on all fours, I launched into the menu of the special Christmas Eve supper to be offered after the service. I told him about the stocking with his name on it, provided by the women's society.

Silence. There was no indication that he either heard or cared about Christmas.

And at last, because I could think of no other way to make contact, I got down on my stomach and wriggled in beside him, bedsprings snagging my suit jacket. For what seemed a long time I lay there with my cheek pressed against the floor. At first I talked about the big wreath above the altar and the candles in the windows. I reminded him of the carol he and the other children were going to sing. Then I ran out of things to say and simply waited there beside him.

And as I waited, a small, chilled hand crept into mine.

"You know, Tommy," I said after a bit, "it's kind of close quarters under here. Let's you and me go out where we can stand up."

And so we did, but slowly, in no hurry. All the pressure had gone from my day, because, you see, I had my Christmas sermon. Flattened there on the floor I realized I had been given a new glimpse of the mystery of this season.

Hadn't God called us, too, as I'd called Tommy, from far above us? With His stars and mountains, His whole majestic creation, hadn't He pleaded with us to love Him, to enjoy the universe He gave us?

And when we would not listen, He had drawn closer. Through prophets and lawgivers and holy men, He spoke with us face-to-face.

But it was not until that first Christmas, until God stooped to earth itself, until He took our very place and came to dwell with us in our loneliness and alienation, that we, like Tommy, dared to stretch out our hands to take hold of love.

—Henry Carter

The Love that Lives

Every child on earth is holy,
Every crib is a manger lowly,
Every home is a stable dim,
Every kind word is a hymn,
Every star is God's own gem,
And every town is Bethlehem,
For Christ is born and born again,
When His love lives in hearts of men.

—W. D. Dorrity

The Empty Room

To us it was such a lovely room, mostly because we created it from a dark, musty parlor, and because before we moved to the farm in our valley, we had never had a spare room for guests.

My husband and I loved to entertain the many guests who came our way. Our two oldest children had married and moved away, but our three young foster daughters kept the house lively and happy.

April 30th was a beautiful day, spring was bursting out all over the valley, dogwood and redbud a riot of glorious color on the mountainside. I felt my cup running over with happiness and contentment as I kissed my husband good-bye and left for my work in town. Two hours later, at my desk in the courtroom, they handed me a note: "Your husband has had a fatal heart attack."

How often had I seen such tragedies come to others and rather smugly offered words of comfort, but there was no more beauty left in that spring for me. A merciful numbness carried me through the next few weeks, my adored husband laid to rest, the farm that meant so much to all of us sold at auction, everything gone but the homeplace, and I knew that would be mine only temporarily.

It was then that an awful cycle of fear and loss of faith began. Spring merged into summer outside, but inside me there was a wall of ice separating me from my Lord as well as from my friends. I tried to make contact with God for release and comfort, but there seemed no communication at all. I can see now, looking back, that it was because each attempted prayer ended, "Why, God? Why me?"

At the time I didn't really want comfort, just to get off by myself and "lick my wounds." This meant shutting out all the love and help offered by caring friends, and as I shut them out I closed the door to the guest room, which Bob and I had labored over so hard to create a place of cheerful hospitality. The room stayed closed the entire summer; there were no guests now to brighten our household. I could not dispel my mood of gloom.

I tried to tell God that I knew He knew best, but I really didn't mean it—I could see no best at all.

Suddenly it was December. Christmas had always been the most important holiday of the year in our home. There was the fun of cutting our own tree, which gave off a fragrant smell of cedar throughout the house. There was all the cooking, fixing and planning that mountain folks do.

But now I couldn't bear the thought of Christmas. I even suggested to my three foster daughters that we not have a tree that year. But my suggestion brought tears and promises that the girls would do everything themselves if I'd just agree. So finally I relented. Their next appeal was for the Christmas party our church's women were to hold at the parsonage, two miles up the valley. For the girls' sake, I decided to force myself to take them, though I didn't want to face it. When snow started falling, I said to them hypocritically, "If you *have* to go, I guess we'll trust the Lord and drive in low gear. Maybe we'll make it."

We made it all right, and the girls were so happy there. But the warmth had not reached my frozen heart. Soon the party was ending, early because the snow was getting heavy. As we were about to leave, a loud knock came at the door. When our hostess opened it, there stood a tall, grim-faced young man, covered with snow.

"Our car has broken down part way up the mountain," he said, "and this was the only light we saw, so we walked down."

It was then that I saw the young woman behind him, her face white and frightened. As we drew them in, offering food and coffee, I saw she was in an advanced stage of pregnancy.

The boy, just home from Vietnam, was on his way to his new post in North Carolina after picking up his wife in Minnesota. He kept telling us that everything they had was inside that car. He was afraid that something might happen to it.

One of the women called a man in the next valley who had a tow truck. She told him of the young couple's plight, and he promised to try to make it over and get the car to a garage, some sixteen miles distant.

As I went into the kitchen for more coffee, I heard one of the women say, "Where can they stay tonight?"

As she spoke, she looked up and saw me. I'll never forget the way her eyes shifted from my face, and the utter silence that followed, but the message was loud and clear. They expected no help from me. Hadn't I shut out even my closest friends for months? They knew they couldn't ask me to help.

And yet, I was the only one with room enough—if only I would share it. The others had children home or company for Christmas, and their homes could not really accommodate the young couple.

No room, I thought.

Then, in that moment, God spoke to me, and I knew, for the first time since my loss, that I had made contact with Him again.

Here was a night such as might have been ages ago—a young man and an expectant mother in deep distress. But, though this was not Bethlehem, wasn't I an innkeeper with a "no vacancy" sign? I had the guest room. It was closed and dark, but this was Christmas. Surely God had sent these visitors out of the storm.

I felt my heart soar as I hustled them into my car, turning to call "Merry Christmas" to my friends. And then we were driving home through the thick, falling snow. It was like driving into a beautiful Christmas card as the car lights picked out the snow-laden firs that lined the narrow road.

"Everywhere, everywhere, Christmas tonight," kept going through my head, and I bubbled over to our young guests about the room that waited for them and how happy we were to have them. When we finally got home I threw open the door to the guest room and flooded it with light. I saw the first smiles of the evening on their faces, the relief of knowing they had sanctuary from the storm and worry.

But the real blessing was mine, for I had opened another door at the same time, my heart's door. I went about the house turning on the lights in each room, as if to transfer some of the light of God's love now flooding my being into those rooms I had made gloomy and sad for so long.

The snowplows did their work in the night, and our young friends were soon on their way the next day. But the happy, almost frenzied activity in our house carried on through Christmas.

Then, in January came a letter from our night visitors:

"We'll never forget you or that lovely, friendly room. Enclosed is a picture of our baby girl I was carrying that night in those snowy mountains. We could see only one little light, but it led us to you."

As I read, happy tears came, and I bowed my head and whispered, "One little light to them, Lord Jesus, one great light for me that opened my heart for the spirit of Christmas to enter and heal my grief.

"Please, God, may every Christmas be as blessed as that one."

—*Betty Banner*

Make a Little Manger

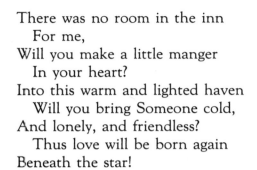

There was no room in the inn
  For me,
Will you make a little manger
  In your heart?
Into this warm and lighted haven
  Will you bring Someone cold,
And lonely, and friendless?
  Thus love will be born again
Beneath the star!

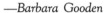

—*Barbara Gooden*

The warmth of Christmas in the family

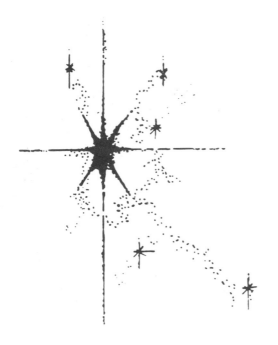

Thou Shalt Know Him
When He Comes

Thou shalt know Him when He comes,
Not by any din of drums,
Nor the vantage of His airs,
Nor by anything He wears;
Neither by His crown,
Nor His gown,
But His presence known shall be
By the holy harmony
Which His coming makes in thee.

—Author Unknown

At Christmas the _____ Heart Goes Home

At Christmas all roads lead home.

The filled planes, packed trains, overflowing buses all speak eloquently of a single destination: home. Despite the crowding and the crushing, the delays, the confusion, we clutch our bright packages and beam our anticipation. We are like birds driven by an instinct we only faintly understand—the hunger to be with our own people.

If we are already snug by our own fireside, surrounded by growing children, or awaiting the return of older ones who are away, then the heart takes a side trip. In memory we journey back to the Christmases of long ago. Once again we are curled into quivering balls of excitement, listening to the mysterious rustle of tissue paper and the tinkle of untold treasures as parents perform their magic on Christmas Eve. Or we recall the special Christmases that are like little landmarks in the life of a family.

One memory is particularly dear to me—a Christmas during the Great Depression when Dad was out of work and the rest of us were scattered, struggling to get through school or simply to survive. My sister, Gwen, and her schoolteacher husband, on his first job in another state, were expecting their first baby. My brother Harold, an aspiring actor, was traveling with a road show. I was a senior working my way through a small college five hundred miles away. My boss had offered me fifty dollars—a fortune!—just to keep the office open the two weeks he and his wife would be gone.

"And boy, do I need the money! Mom, I know you'll understand," I wrote.

I wasn't prepared for her brave if wistful reply. The other kids couldn't make it either! Except for my kid brother, Barney, she and Dad would be alone. "This house is going to seem empty, but don't worry—we'll be okay."

I did worry, though. Our first Christmas apart! And as the carols drifted up the stairs, as the corridors rang with the laughter and chatter of other girls packing up to leave, my misery deepened.

Then one night when the dorm was almost empty I had a long-distance call. "Gwen!" I gasped. "What's wrong?" (Long-distance usually meant an emergency back in those days.)

"Listen, Leon's got a new generator and we think the old jalopy can make it home. I've wired Harold—if he can meet us halfway, he can ride with us. But don't tell the folks; we want to surprise them. Marj, you've just got to come, too."

"But I haven't got a dime for presents!"

"Neither have we. Cut up a catalogue and bring pictures of all the goodies you'd buy if you could—and will someday!"

"I could do *that,* Gwen. But I just can't leave here now."

When we hung up I reached for the scissors. Furs and perfume. Wrist watches, clothes, cars—how all of us longed to lavish beautiful things on those we loved. Well, at least I could mail mine home—with IOUs.

I was still dreaming over this "wish list" when I was called to the phone again. It was my boss, saying he'd decided to close the office after all. My heart leaped up, for if it wasn't too late to catch a ride as far as Fort Dodge with the girl down the hall . . . ! I ran to pound on her door.

They already had a load, she said—but if I was willing to sit on somebody's lap . . . Her dad was downstairs waiting. I threw things into a suitcase, then rammed a hand down the torn lining of my coat sleeve so fast it emerged mittened and I had to start over.

It was snowing as we piled into that heaterless car. We drove all night with the side curtains flapping, singing and hugging each other to keep warm. Not minding—how could we? We were going home!

"Marj!" Mother stood at the door, clutching her robe about her, silver-black hair spilling down her back, eyes large with alarm, then incredulous joy. "Oh . . . *Marj.*"

I'll never forget those eyes or the feel of her arms around me, so soft and warm after the bitter cold. My feet felt frozen after that all-night drive, but they warmed up as my parents fed me and put me to bed. And when I woke up hours later it was to the jangle of sleigh bells Dad hung on the door each year. And voices. My kid brother shouting, "Harold! Gwen!" The clamor of astonished greetings, the laughter, the kissing, the questions. And we all gathered around the kitchen table the way we used to, recounting our adventures.

"I had to hitchhike clear to Peoria," my older brother scolded merrily. "Me, the leading man . . ." He lifted an elegant two-toned shoe—with a flapping sole—"In these!"

"But by golly, you *got* here." Dad's chubby face was beaming. Then suddenly he broke down—Dad, who never cried. "We're together!"

Together. The best present we could give one another, we realized. All of us. Just being here in the old house where we'd shared so many Christmases. No gifts on our lavish lists, if they could materialize, could equal that.

In most Christmases since that memorable one we've been lucky. During the years our children were growing up there were no separations. Then one year, appallingly, history repeated itself. For valid reasons, not a single faraway child could get home. Worse, my husband had flown to Florida for some vital surgery. A proud, brave man—he was adamant about our not coming with him "just because it's Christmas," when he'd be back in another week.

Like my mother before me, I still had one lone chick left—Melanie, fourteen. "We'll get along fine," she said, trying to cheer me.

We built a big fire every evening, went to church, wrapped presents, pretended. But the ache in our hearts kept swelling. And, the day before Christmas, we burst into mutual tears. "Mommy, it's just not *right* for Daddy to be down there alone!"

"I know it." Praying for a miracle, I ran to the telephone. The airlines were hopeless, but there was one roomette available on the last train to Miami. Almost hysterical with relief, we threw things into bags.

And what a Christmas Eve! Excited as conspirators, we cuddled together in that cozy space. Melanie hung a tiny wreath in the window and we settled down to watch the endless pageantry flashing by to the rhythmic clicking song of the rails . . . Little villages and city streets—all dancing with lights and decorations and sparkling Christmas trees . . . And cars and snowy countrysides and people—all the people. Each one on his or her special pilgrimage of love and celebration this precious night.

At last we drifted off to sleep. But hours later I awoke to a strange stillness. The train had stopped. And raising the shade, I peered out on a very small town. Silent, deserted, with only a few lights still burning. And under the bare branches, along a lonely street, a figure was walking. A young man in sailor blues, head bent, hunched under the weight of the sea bag on his shoulders. And I thought—*home! Poor kid, he's almost home.* And I wondered if there was someone still up waiting for him; or if anyone knew he was coming at all. And my heart cried out to him, for he was suddenly my own son—and my own ghost, and the soul of us all—driven, so immutably driven by this annual call, "Come home!"

Home for Christmas. There must be some deep psychological reason why we turn so instinctively toward home at this special time. Perhaps we are acting out the ancient story of a man and a woman and a coming child, plodding along with their donkey toward their destination. It was necessary for Joseph, the earthly father, to go home to be taxed. Each male had to return to the city of his birth.

Birth. The tremendous miracle of birth shines through every step and syllable of the Bible story. The long, arduous trip across the mountains of Galilee and Judea was also the journey of a *life* toward birth. Mary was already in labor when they arrived in Bethlehem, so near the time of her delivery that in desperation, since the inn was full, her husband settled for a humble stable.

The Child Who was born on that first Christmas grew up to be a man. Jesus. He healed many people, taught us many important things. But the message that has left the most lasting impression and given the most hope and comfort is this: that we do have a home to go to, and there will be an ultimate homecoming. A place where we will indeed be reunited with those we love.

Anyway, that's my idea of Heaven. A place where Mother is standing in the door, probably bossing Dad the way she used to about the turkey or the tree, and he's enjoying every minute of it. And old friends and neighbors are streaming in and out and the sense of love and joy and celebration will go on forever.

A place where every day will be Christmas, with everybody there together. At home.

—*Marjorie Holmes*

My Most Memorable Christmas

Why is one Christmas more memorable than another?

It seldom has anything to do with material gifts. In fact, poor circumstances often bring out the creativity in a family.

But I think the most memorable Christmases are tied in somehow with family milestones: reunions, separations, births and, yes, even death. Perhaps that is why Christmas, 1960, stands out so vividly in my memory.

We spent that Christmas at Evergreen Farm in Lincoln, Virginia—the home of my parents. With us were my sister and her husband—Emmy and Harlow Hoskins—and their two girls, Lynn and Winifred. It meant a typical family occasion with our three children, Linda, Chester and Jeffrey, along with Peter John who was then a senior at Yale. Five children can make an old farmhouse ring with the yuletide spirit.

For our Christmas Eve service, Lynn and Linda had prepared an improvised altar before the living room fireplace. Jeffrey and Winifred (the youngest grandchildren) lighted all the candles. Then with all of his family gathered around him, my father read Luke's incomparable account of the first Christmas. There was carol singing, with Chester and Winifred singing a duet, "Hark, the Herald Angels Sing," in their high piping voices. Then my mother, the storyteller of the family, gave us an old favorite, "Why the Chimes Rang." She made us see the ragged little boy creeping up that long cathedral aisle and slipping his gift onto the altar.

Then she said, "You know, I'd like to make a suggestion to the family. The floor underneath the tree in the den is piled high with gifts we're giving to one another. But we're celebrating Christ's birthday—not each other's. This is His time of year. What are we going to give to Jesus?"

The room began to hum with voices comparing notes. But Mother went on, "Let's think about it for a few moments. Then we'll go around the circle and each of us will tell what gift he or she will lay on the altar for Christ's birthday."

Chester, age seven, crept close to his father for a whispered consultation. Then he said shyly, "What I'd like to give Jesus this year is not to lose my temper anymore."

Jeffrey, age four, who had been slow in night training, was delightfully specific: "I'll give Him my diapers."

Winifred said softly that she was going to give Jesus good grades in school. Len's was, "To be a better father, which means a gift of more patience."

And so it went . . . on around the group. Peter John's was short but significant. "What I want to give to Christ is a more dedicated life." I was to remember that statement five years later at the moment of his ordination into the Presbyterian ministry when he stood so straight and so tall and answered so resoundingly, "I do so believe . . . I do so promise. . . ." Yet at Christmastime, 1960, the ministry was probably the last thing he expected to get into.

Then it was my father's turn. "I certainly don't want to inject too solemn a note into this," he said, "but somehow I know that this is the last Christmas I'll be sitting in this room with my family gathered around me like this."

We gasped and protested, but he would not be stopped. "No, I so much want to say this. I've had a most wonderful life. Long, long ago I gave my life to Christ. Though I've tried to serve Him, I've failed Him often. But He has blessed me with great riches—especially my family. I want to say this while you're all here. I may not have another chance. Even after I go on into the next life, I'll still be with you. And, of course, I'll be waiting for each one of you there."

There was love in his brown eyes—and tears in ours. No one said anything for a moment. Time seemed to stand still in the quiet room. Firelight and candlelight played on the children's faces as they looked at their grandfather, trying to grasp what he was saying. The fragrance of balsam and cedar was in the air. The old windowpanes reflected back the red glow of Christmas lights.

Father did leave this world four months later—on May 1st. His passing was like a benediction. It happened one afternoon as he sat quietly in a chair in the little village post office, talking to some of his friends. His heart just stopped beating. That Christmas Eve he had known with a strange sureness that the time was close.

Every time I think of Father now, I can see that scene in the living room—like a jewel of a moment set in the ordinary moments that make up our days. For that brief time real values came clearly into focus: Father's gratitude for life; Mother's strong faith; my husband's quiet strength; my son's inner yearning momentarily shining through blurred youthful ambitions; the eager faces of children groping toward understanding and truth; the reality of the love of God as our thoughts focused on Him Whose birth we were commemorating.

It was my most memorable Christmas.

—*Catherine Marshall*

Mother's Last Christmas

We lived on a farm in the mountains of Virginia, and for many years my mother made her home with us. But one morning Mother woke up completely disoriented, and during the years that followed, she grew progressively worse. Her ability to communicate with anyone was gone. I felt numb about her silent condition, as though she were lost to us and, it seemed to me, lost to God as well.

On the day before Christmas Eve some carolers came over the hills. The group of young people—led by Miss Winnie and Miss Naomi, two missionaries from our church, and our pastor's wife, Phyllis—sang in the snow outside our door. Then I hustled everyone into our big, warm kitchen for hot chocolate and cookies. I took the three ladies into Mother's room, and Phyllis leaned over the bed and said, "Grandmother, it's Christmas."

No response.

Phyllis took her hand and said again, "Grandmother, do you know what Christmas is?"

Then it happened. Mother's eyes flew open, and it was as if a light had been turned on behind them; an angelic smile spread over her worn features, and in a strong, normal voice she replied, "Oh, yes! It is the birthday of my precious Savior."

Now we eagerly plied Mother with questions, but it was over. Those were the last words that Mother ever spoke, but they were enough. I knew beyond a shadow of a doubt that the birth of Jesus Christ has a power beyond anything we can consciously comprehend. And that Mother was in His hands forever.

—*Betty Banner*

The Year We Had a "Sensible" Christmas

For as long as I could remember our family had talked about a sensible Christmas. Every year, my mother would limp home from shopping or she would sit beside the kitchen table after hours of baking, close her eyes, catch her breath and say, "This is the last time I'm going to exhaust myself with all this holiday fuss. Next year we're going to have a *sensible* Christmas."

And always my father, if he was within earshot, would agree. "It's not worth the time and expense."

While we were kids, my sister and I lived in dread that Mom and Dad would go through with their rash vows of a reduced Christmas. But if they ever *did*, we reasoned, there were several things about Christmas that we ourselves would like to amend. And two of these were, namely, my mother's Uncle Lloyd and his wife, Aunt Amelia.

Many a time Lizzie and I wondered why families had to have relatives, and especially why it was our fate to inherit Uncle Lloyd and Aunt Amelia. They were a sour and a formal pair who came to us every Christmas, bringing Lizzie and me handkerchiefs as gifts and expecting in return silence, respect, service and for me to surrender my bedroom.

Lizzie and I had understood early that Great-uncle Lloyd was, indeed, a poor man, and we were sympathetic to this. But we dared to think that even poverty provided no permit for them to be stiff and unwarm and a nuisance in the bargain. Still we accepted Great-uncle Lloyd and Great-aunt Amelia as our lot and they were, for years, as much the tradition of Christmas as mistletoe.

Then came my first year in college. It must have been some perverse reaction to my being away, but Mom started it. *This* was to be the year of the sensible Christmas. "By not exhausting ourselves with all the folderol," she wrote me, "we'll at last have the energy and the time to appreciate Christmas."

Dad, as usual, went along with Mom, but added his own touch. We were not to spend more than a dollar for each of our gifts to one another. "For once," Dad said, "we'll worry about the thought behind the gift, and not about its price."

It was I who suggested that our sensible Christmas be limited to the immediate family, just the four of us. The motion was carried. Mom wrote a gracious letter to Great-uncle Lloyd explaining that what with my being away in school and for one reason and another we weren't going to do much about Christmas, so maybe they would enjoy it more if they didn't make their usual great effort to come. Dad enclosed a check, an unexpected boon.

I arrived home from college that Christmas wondering what to expect. A wreath on the front door provided a fitting nod to the season. There was a Christmas tree in the living room and I must admit that, at first, it made my heart twinge. Artificial, the tree was small and seemed without character when compared to the luxurious, forest-smelling firs of former years. But the more I looked at it, with our brightly wrapped dollar gifts under it, the friendlier it became and I began to think of the mess of real trees, and their fire threat, and how ridiculous, how really unnatural it was to bring a living tree inside a house anyway. Already the idea of a sensible Christmas was getting to me.

Christmas Eve Mom cooked a good but simple dinner and afterward we all sat together in the living room. "This is nice," Lizzie purred, a-snuggle in the big cabbage rose chair.

"Yes," Dad agreed. "It's quiet. I'm not tired out. For once, I think I can stay awake until church."

"If this were last Christmas," I reminded Mom, "you'd still be in the kitchen with your hours of last-minute jobs. More cookies. More fruit cake." I recalled the compulsive way I used to nibble at Mom's fruit cake. "But I never really liked it," I confessed with a laugh.

"I didn't know that," Mom said. She was thoughtful for a moment. Then her face brightened. "But Aunt Amelia—how *she* adored it!"

"Maybe she was just being nice," Lizzie said undiplomatically.

Then we fell silent. Gradually we took to reading. Dad did slip off into a short snooze before church.

Christmas morning we slept late, and once up we breakfasted before advancing to our gifts. And what a time we had with those! We laughed merrily at our own originality and cleverness. I gave Mom a cluster-pin that I had fashioned out of aluminum measuring spoons and had adorned with rhinestones. Mother wore the pin all day or, at least, until we went out to Dempsey's.

At Dempsey's, the best restaurant in town, we had a wonderful, unrushed feast. There was only one awkward moment just after the consommé was served. We started to lift our spoons. Then Dad suggested that we say grace and we all started to hold hands around the table as we always do at home, and then we hesitated and drew our hands back, and then in unison we refused to be intimidated by a public eating place and held hands and said grace.

Nothing much happened the rest of the day. In the evening I wandered into the kitchen, opened the refrigerator, poked around for a minute, closed the door and came back to the living room.

"That's a joke," I reported, with no idea at all of the effect my next remark would have. "I went out to pick at the turkey."

In tones that had no color, Mother spoke. "I knew that's what you went out there for. I've been waiting for it to happen."

No longer could she stay the sobs that now burst forth from her. "Kate!" Dad cried, rushing to her.

"Forgive me. Forgive me," Mom kept muttering.

"For what, dear? Please tell us."

"For this terrible, dreadful, sensible Christmas."

Each of us knew what she meant. Our Christmas had been as artificial as that Christmas tree; at some point the spirit of the day had just quietly crept away from us. In our efforts at common sense we had lost the reason for Christmas and had forgotten about others; this denied Him Whose birthday it was all about. Each of us, we knew full well, had contributed to this selfishness, but Mom was taking the blame.

As her sobs became sniffles and our assurances began to take effect, Mom addressed us more coherently, in Mom's own special incoherent way. "I should have been in the kitchen last night instead of wasting my time," she began, covering up her sentimentality with anger. "So you don't like my fruit cake, Harry? Too bad. Aunt Amelia *really* adores it! And Elizabeth, even if she doesn't, you shouldn't be disrespectful to the old soul. Do you know who else loves my fruit cake? Mrs. Donegan down the street loves it. And she didn't get her gift from me this year. Why? Because we're being *sensible.*" Then Mom turned on Dad, wagging her finger at him. "We can't afford to save on Christmas, Lewis! It shuts off the heart."

That seemed to sum it up.

Yet, Lizzie had another way of saying it. She put it in a letter to me at school, a letter as lovely as Lizzie herself. "Mom feels," Lizzie wrote, "that the strains and stresses are the birth pangs of Christmas. So do I. I'm certain that it is out of our efforts and tiredness and turmoil that some sudden, quiet, shining, priceless thing occurs each year and if all we produce is only a feeling as long as a flicker, it is worth the bother."

Just as my family came to call that The Christmas That Never Was, the next one became the Prodigal Christmas. It was the most festive, and the most frazzling time in our family's history—not because we spent any more money, but because we threw all of ourselves into the joy of Christmas. In the woods at the edge of town we cut the largest tree we'd ever had. Lizzie and I swathed the house in greens. Delicious smells came from the kitchen as Mom baked and baked and baked. . . . We laughed and sang carols and joked. Even that dour pair, Great-uncle Lloyd and Great-aunt Amelia, were almost, but not quite, gay. Still, it was through them that I felt that quick surge of warmth, that glorious "feeling as long as a flicker," that made Christmas meaningful.

We had just sat down in our own dining room and had reached out our hands to one another for our circle of grace. When I took Great-aunt Amelia's hand in mine, it happened. I learned something about her and about giving that, without this Christmas, I might never have known.

The hand that I held was cold. I became aware of how gnarled her fingers were, how years of agonizing arthritis had twisted them. Only then did I think of the handkerchiefs that Lizzie and I had received this year, as in all the years before. For the first time I saw clearly the delicate embroidery, the painstaking needlework—Great-aunt Amelia's yearly gift of love to, and for, us.

—*Henry Appers*

Homemade Holy Night

Where did I get the idea of a family Christmas pageant? I don't really know. All I can say is that when the idea came to me, I felt that I might never see a Christmas again.

It was June. I'd just gone through major cancer surgery that hadn't been fully successful. Once a month I'd travel two hundred fifty miles to Houston for chemotherapy, and returning home I felt sick to death.

The days were long. My husband, Gene, is a telephone repairman, and we live on a hilltop in the farm country of central Texas. It's beautiful country, but I had no energy to go out in it. I'd just sit by the window and watch our horse loping from the barn to the shade of the mulberry tree. I'd lost my appetite, my hair, but, worst of all, at times I was too sick to *care* whether or not I got well.

My family tried to bolster my spirits, but I couldn't seem to focus on anything. Then I tried playing a little game with myself. "Get rid of all those gloomy thoughts, Ella Ruth," I told myself. "Start thinking only good, bright thoughts." And when I asked myself what was good and bright, I came up with—Christmas, my favorite time of year.

If only, I thought, *if only I could feel that every day was leading me nearer and nearer to Christmas.*

But what could I do? Start my Christmas shopping early? In summer? No, that would be silly. Well, maybe I could plan a special celebration that would bring my family all together. And, of course, it should honor Jesus' birth. I had read somewhere that cancer patients should set goals—and a Christ-honoring Christmas became one of my goals.

What I really wanted to do was bring the Christmas story to life for my grandchildren. Maybe a Christmas play. . . .

Yes! But how? Where? With what? My mind and body were weak. How could I put a play together?

I prayed, "Father, I want to honor You, but You'll have to show me how. I don't even know where to start."

Slowly God got me going. Looking out the window, I saw our barn and thought, *There! There's the manger, Ella Ruth.*

I knew what the plot of the play should be—it was right there in Luke.

Then I wondered who in my family could play what parts? Right away I saw that we had a perfect Mary. My daughter, Kristi, was pregnant, due in February . . . and her husband, Bobby, had a beard. He could be Joseph. The angels and shepherds? My grandchildren.

There was my cast. But what would we do? Stand around in the barn? No. Somehow I would have to come up with a simple script, and so I studied Luke 2 and Christmas books for ideas.

And costumes. Did I have the needed strength to make them? I really didn't want anybody's help. I wanted this to be a secret between the Lord and me.

"Go slow," I heard God saying, "and I'll help you." I did take it slow. During my long afternoons, I would sit beside our old cedar trunk, rummaging through mementos of wonderful times.

There was an old jeweled collar . . . how stylish I'd felt wearing this in the long-ago days when my husband and I were courting. Now the collar could be a Wise Man's crown. A red-and-black afghan . . . here was a labor of love. My daughter, Kristi, had made this for me just before her marriage. Now it could keep warm a king of the Orient. Old elastic hairbands and old towels—sewn together they'd make head-dresses for the shepherds.

My house took on new life, with all the objects in it calling out to be used.

One day, though, while turning a pillowcase into a shepherd's dress, I suddenly suffered doubts. Was I setting myself up for a big embarrassment? What if my children and grandchildren thought this was a stupid, silly idea? Would six-year-old Jeremy take one look at his pillowcase and say, "Forget it"?

But the longer I thought, the more sure I was that my family—they were all a bunch of "actors," anyway—would play along wholeheartedly. So I hoped.

A month before the holiday, I let my husband, Gene, in on my secret. I needed him to make the "star in the East" and shepherds' crooks in his workshop. And when we made the drive to Houston for my chemotherapy, the fear and silence were a little less terrible. Gene and I had pageant details to talk about.

Then, before I knew it, the holiday was upon us. I arranged to have all of our family gather at our house for Christmas Eve. They suspected something when I told them to wear warm clothes.

All was going well until the day before, when a heavy rain began to fall. Would we be able to get to the manger in the barn? I forlornly painted a king's crown, and looked up now and then to see the rain come pouring down.

The morning of Christmas Eve, though, we woke up to a clear sky and a brisk north wind. By noon, the way to the manger was dry.

During Christmas Eve dinner, I was a bundle of joyous nerves. I could barely eat. As everyone began the after-dinner cleanup, Gene and I exchanged winks and then he slipped outside to set up the star and arrange things in the barn.

Dishes done, everyone gathered around me, waiting for me to spill my secret. But my doubts were back. Would everyone try to back out? Handing out costumes and printed instructions, I didn't dare look up to see how everyone was reacting. But then my son Mike quietly said, "Hey, Ma, I haven't seen you this excited since . . . in a long time."

I felt I'd just been given a big dose of bravery. When everyone was dressed, I began to read from Luke 2 and the pageant at last began to unfold. Joseph and Mary ("being great with child") left the house and I told of their journey to Bethlehem. With no room at the inn, they took refuge in the barn. We then watched from the window as shepherds went out into the field. My daughter-in-law Donna wore an old quilt top and a towel headdress and her little Jeremy and Kerrie wore old pillowcases.

Then, "the angel of the Lord [my oldest grandchild] came upon them." Tracy was wrapped in a white bedsheet, with a tinsel halo nestled in her hair. I flipped a light switch and "the glory of the Lord shone round about them." More angels, little Kellie (Kerrie's twin sister) and Stephanie, appeared. The angels brought "good tidings of great joy" to the shepherds, and then they all headed for the manger. I followed, leaving the Wise Men in the house.

In the barn everything was dark, except for a gentle glow shining on Mary, Joseph and the Babe (a doll) in swaddling clothes. Angels and shepherds and my husband kneeled or stood in the shadows, silent in the cold night air.

I stood at the door and read the story of the Wise Men from Matthew 2. My husband's handmade "star in the east," a flashlight hidden within a cardboard star, began moving along its cable toward the barn. The Wise Men (my two sons, Ron and Mike, and our family friend David Taylor) followed the star across the field, singing "We Three Kings of Orient Are."

And then the Wise Men were with us, in their jeweled and (bath)-robed splendor, presenting their gifts as an angel sang "Silent Night." Then the grandchildren sang "Away in a Manger." We all joined in on "Joy to the World."

This was all I had planned. But none of us could move. We all felt God's warm presence in this cold, dark barn.

My oldest son, Ron, gently broke the stillness, saying, "I feel like we should pray." Ron led us in a prayer of praise, and we then sang another carol, and then another, all of us wanting to hang on a little longer to this loving closeness.

And in that closeness I no longer felt like the sick one in the family—I simply felt like one of the family. A good loving family. I'd left my fear behind. My soul was full of light, a newborn light that God had been leading me to for six months. It was the radiance of the manger, a radiance I'd helped God create.

So you see, if you're stricken by illness or misfortune, set some goals. Find something worthwhile to do. And then *do* it. Make a Christmas pageant or an Easter vigil or organize a bake sale. If you know a trade, offer your services to those in need. To get better, you often have to go out of your way. Don't be afraid. Go.

—*Ella Ruth Rettig*

The Gift of Sharing _____

It was Christmas Eve, 1933. Mama was preparing to bake her "hard-times fruitcake," so called because the only similarity to fruit it contained was prunes. But it was, to our family, an extra-special cake. My sisters, Lottie, Vivian, Estelle and Dolly, and I sat around our kitchen table, shelling pecans for the cake.

None of us, except Mama, was enthusiastic, and I suspected her gaiety was partly put on. "Mama," I asked, "why can't Grandma and Aunt Ella, and Aunt Fran and Uncle Hugh, and all the cousins come for Christmas like last year? We won't even have any music unless Joe comes and brings his guitar."

We wouldn't mind not having a Christmas tree because we'd never had one, and Mama and Daddy had prepared us for the possibility of no presents, but the thought of no visitors or music really subdued us. Dolly, age five and the youngest, sobbed.

"Why'd we have to move, anyway?" she asked, sniffling. So Mama again explained her version of Dust Bowl economics.

"When we had to give up our farm, we were lucky to find this place to rent, even if it is too far for the relatives to come. Don't worry, though," Mama reassured us. "Why, God might send us company for Christmas right out of the blue, if we believe strong enough." She began to pit the boiled prunes and mash them.

As we worked, a wind came up and whistled through the newspaper we'd stuffed into the cracks in the corners. A cold gust blasted us as Daddy entered through the back door after doing the chores at the barn. "It looks like we're in for a blue norther," he said, rubbing his hands together.

Later, Daddy built up a roaring cow chip and mesquite fire in the potbellied stove in the living room, and we were about to get into our flannel nightgowns when someone knocked on the door. A traveler, wrapped in his bedroll, had missed the main road and stopped to ask for shelter from the storm for the night.

"Mind you," he said, when he'd had a cup of hot coffee, "I don't take charity. I work for my keep. I'm headed for California. Heard there's work to be had there."

Then Mama fixed our visitor a cozy pallet behind the stove. We girls went into our bedroom and all crawled into the same bed for warmth. "Reckon he's the one Mama said God might send out of the blue for Jesus' birthday?" I whispered.

"He must be. Who else'd be out in weather like this?" Lottie said, and Vivian and Estelle agreed. We snuggled, pondered and slept.

At breakfast our guest sopped biscuits in gravy. "I never had a family that I remember," he said. "Can't recollect any name 'cept Gibson. You can call me Mr. Gibson if you want." He smiled, revealing gums without teeth. Seemingly, he had no possessions beyond his bedroll and the clothes he wore, but he pulled a large harmonica from his pants pocket and said, "I've always had this. Want me to play something?"

So Mr. Gibson spent Christmas Day with us, and what a delight he was! He helped with the work, told us stories and played all the beloved Christmas songs on his harmonica. He played by ear as we sang church hymns. After much pleading on our part, he agreed to stay one more night.

The next morning, when we awakened, Mr. Gibson was gone. I found his harmonica on the kitchen table. "Oh, Mama," I cried, "Mr. Gibson forgot his harmonica—the only thing he had."

Mama looked thoughtful. "No," she said softly. She picked it up and ran her palm over the curlicues etched in the metal sides. "I think he left it on purpose."

"Oh, I see," I said, "sort of a Christmas present. And we didn't give him anything."

"Yes, we did, honey. We gave him a family for Christmas," she said, and smiled.

We never saw Mr. Gibson again. Daddy had an ear for music and quickly learned to play the harmonica. Through the years, it brought many a joyful memory of that unforgettable Christmas when God sent us Mr. Gibson right out of the blue—a blue norther, that is—because He knew how much a man with music, who longed for a family, and a family without music, who longed for company, needed each other.

—Doris Crandall

Christmas Everywhere

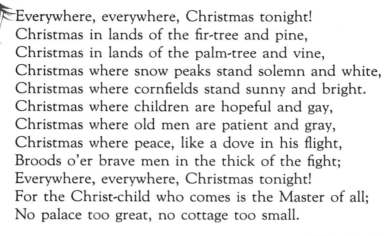

Everywhere, everywhere, Christmas tonight!
Christmas in lands of the fir-tree and pine,
Christmas in lands of the palm-tree and vine,
Christmas where snow peaks stand solemn and white,
Christmas where cornfields stand sunny and bright.
Christmas where children are hopeful and gay,
Christmas where old men are patient and gray,
Christmas where peace, like a dove in his flight,
Broods o'er brave men in the thick of the fight;
Everywhere, everywhere, Christmas tonight!
For the Christ-child who comes is the Master of all;
No palace too great, no cottage too small.

—Phillips Brooks

The wonder
of Christmas
and children

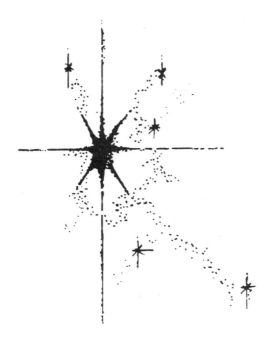

As a Little Child

Christmas is a child's day,
(O, my heart keep young.)
Christmas is the loveliest
Song a child has sung.
Christmas is the starriest
Night of joy and mirth.
Every little child is glad
That Jesus came to earth.
Christmas is a child's day,
Watch a child's eyes shine!
(Heavenly Father, let me keep
The Christmas light in mine.)
Christmas is so holy,
Pure and clean and white—
(Heavenly Father, let me be
A little child tonight.)

—*Grace Noll Crowell*

Waiting...
Waiting for Christmas

Herman and I finally locked our store and dragged ourselves home to South Caldwell Street in Charlotte, North Carolina. It was 11:00 P.M., Christmas Eve of 1949. We were dog tired.

Ours was one of those big old general appliance stores that sold everything from refrigerators and toasters and record players to bicycles and dollhouses and games. We'd sold almost all of our toys; and all of the layaways, except one package, had been picked up.

Usually Herman and I kept the store open until everything had been picked up. We knew we wouldn't have woken up very happy on Christmas morning knowing that some little child's gift was back on the layaway shelf. But the person who had put a dollar down on that package never appeared.

Early Christmas morning our twelve-year-old son, Tom, and Herman and I were out under the tree opening up gifts. But I'll tell you, there was something very humdrum about this Christmas. Tom was growing up; he hadn't wanted any toys—just clothes and games. I missed his childish exuberance of past years.

As soon as breakfast was over, Tom left to visit his friend next door. And Herman disappeared into the bedroom, mumbling, "I'm going back to sleep. There's nothing left to stay up for anyway."

So there I was alone, doing the dishes and feeling very let down. It was nearly 9:00 A.M., and sleet mixed with snow cut the air outside. The wind rattled our windows, and I felt grateful for the warmth of the apartment. *Sure glad I don't have to go out on a day like today,* I thought to myself, picking up the wrappings and ribbons strewn around the living room.

And then it began. Something I'd never experienced before. A strange, persistent urge. "Go to the store," it seemed to say.

I looked at the icy sidewalk outside. *That's crazy,* I said to myself. I tried dismissing the thought, but it wouldn't leave me alone. *Go to the store.*

Well, I *wasn't* going to go. I'd never gone to the store on Christmas Day in all the ten years we'd owned it. No one opened shop on that day. There wasn't any reason to go, I didn't want to, and I wasn't going to.

For an hour, I fought that strange feeling. Finally, I couldn't stand it any longer, and I got dressed.

"Herman," I said, feeling silly, "I think I'll walk down to the store."

Herman woke up with a start. "Whatever for? What are you going to do there?"

"Oh, I don't know," I replied lamely. "There's not much to do here. I just think I'll wander down."

He argued against it a little, but I told him that I'd be back soon. "Well, go on," he grumped, "but I don't see any reason for it."

I put on my gray wool coat and a gray tam on my head, then my galoshes and my red scarf and gloves. Once outside, none of these garments seemed to help. The wind cut right through me and the sleet stung my cheeks. I groped my way along the mile down to 117 East Park Avenue, slipping and sliding all the way.

I shivered, and tucked my hands inside the pockets of my coat to keep them from freezing. I felt ridiculous. I had no business being out in that bitter chill.

There was the store just ahead. The sign announced Radio-Electronic Sales and Service, and the big glass windows jutted out onto the sidewalk. *But, what in the world?* I wondered. In front of the store stood two little boys, huddled together, one about nine, and the other six.

"Here she comes!" yelled the older one. He had his arm around the younger. "See, I told you she would come," he said jubilantly.

They were little black children, and they were half frozen. The younger one's face was wet with tears, but when he saw me, his eyes opened wide and his sobbing stopped.

"What are you two children doing out here in this freezing rain?" I scolded, hurrying them into the store and turning up the heat. "You should be at home on a day like this!" They were poorly dressed. They had no hats or gloves, and their shoes barely held together. I rubbed their small, icy hands, and got them up close to the heater.

"We've been waiting for you," replied the older. They had been standing outside since 9:00 A.M., the time I normally open the store.

"Why were you waiting for me?" I asked, astonished.

"My little brother, Jimmy, didn't get any Christmas." He touched Jimmy's shoulder. "We want to buy some skates. That's what he wants.

We have these three dollars. See, Miss Lady," he said, pulling the money from his pocket.

I looked at the dollars in his hand. I looked at their expectant faces. And then I looked around the store. "I'm sorry," I said, "but we've sold almost everything. We have no ska—" Then my eye caught sight of the layaway shelf with its one lone package. I tried to remember . . . could it be . . . ?

"Wait a minute," I told the boys. I walked over, picked up the package, unwrapped it and, miracle of miracles, there was a pair of skates!

Jimmy reached for them. *Lord,* I said silently, *let them be his size.*

And miracle added upon miracle, they *were* his size.

When the older boy finished tying the laces on Jimmy's right foot and saw that the skate fit—perfectly—he stood up and presented the dollars to me.

"No, I'm not going to take your money," I told him. I *couldn't* take his money. "I want you to have these skates, and I want you to use your money to get some gloves for your hands."

The two boys just blinked at first. Then their eyes became like saucers, and their grins stretched wide when they understood I was giving them the skates, and I didn't want their three dollars.

What I saw in Jimmy's eyes was like a blessing. It was pure joy, and it was beautiful. My low spirits rose.

After the children had warmed up, I turned down the heater, and we walked out together. As I locked the door, I turned to the older brother and said, "How lucky that I happened to come along when I did. If you'd stood there much longer, you'd have frozen. But how did you boys know I would come?"

I wasn't prepared for his reply. His gaze was steady, and he answered me softly. "I knew you would come," he said. "I asked Jesus to send you."

The tingles in my spine weren't from the cold, I knew. God had planned this.

As we waved good-bye, I turned home to a brighter Christmas than I had left. Tom brought his friend over to our house. Herman got out of bed; his father, "Papa" English, and sister, Ella, came by. We had a wonderful dinner and a wonderful time.

But the one thing that made that Christmas really wonderful was the one thing that makes every Christmas wonderful—Jesus was there.

—*Elizabeth English*

The Gift That Kept Giving ___

Eleven years ago, on Christmas Eve, our little girls gave us a unique gift—so unique that it keeps on giving, year after year.

Julie and Jennifer were six and eight. Our twin sons, Jon and Jeremy, were not yet two. I remember I was tired. The boys had required constant attention. Still, I'd done all the things that I always did at Christmas. The tall tree was decorated, the gifts elaborately wrapped. The cooking was done. The door was decorated. Presents for the children had been carefully selected.

I was tired but happy. Julie stopped me in the kitchen. "Mama, Jennifer and I have a present for you and Daddy. It's not something you can wrap up. We want you and Daddy to sit on the sofa and hold the boys, so we can give it to you." I had a few more last-minute things to do, and I really didn't want to sit just then. "Please, Mama," Julie pleaded, "it'll only take a few minutes." I relented and called my husband. It took some doing to get the boys settled in our laps. Finally, though, we were ready for the gift. Julie and Jennifer stood nervously on the hearth, holding hands. They wore red flannel granny gowns with little matching dust caps. "First, we have to turn out the lights," Julie said in a hushed voice. "We just want the Christmas lights from the tree to shine," Jennifer explained.

Looking straight ahead, they sang "Silent Night." Then Julie recited a poem about the love of God. After she finished, Julie asked her Daddy, shyly, "Will you please read us the Christmas story from the Bible, about Jesus getting born? Our Sunday school teacher read it last Sunday."

Jerry got his Bible and read the story, leaning toward the tree so he could see. We all listened. Even the twins were quiet and sat still.

When he finished, Julie asked so softly we could barely hear her, "Now can we pray together?"

We'd never really had family devotions and we weren't sure how to start the prayer. But, nevertheless, a little self-consciously, we prayed, each of us, one at a time. I knew then that something very special was happening to our family. From our daughters' gift, we had learned that we could pray together. So, through the years we continued having devotions, not just at Christmastime, but all through the year.

Our little daughters' gift to the family, on that long-ago Christmas Eve, was the gift of faith. It has grown and supported our family ever since. It's a gift that keeps on giving.

—*Marion Bond West*

The Night We Found Christmas

The toy catalogs began arriving in early October. It was then that I began to fear that I was losing my son Matthew to the merchants of Christmas.

He was eight years old and his brother, Jonathan—"J.J." we call him—had just turned two. Sometimes J.J. leafed through one or another of the catalogs, but mostly it was Matthew who pored over them, dreaming aloud and making known his wishes and, often, demands. Thumbing through the toy-filled pages, circling the items he wanted, seemed to occupy most of his time.

Since my divorce, I had tried to keep Christmas as close as possible to all the others Matthew remembered: full of hope and wonder and excitement. But as November became December, it was clear that this Christmas wasn't quite making it. The outward signs were there, all right. We had the tree up early, a wreath hanging on the front door.

But Matthew seemed hypnotized by the catalogs. Every day, after school and homework, they'd be lugged out to the kitchen table and the monotonous "I want, I want" would begin. It was like a chant that grew louder and more forceful with every toy added to the list.

At first I paid little attention to it. Then one afternoon the intensity of his desire for "things" started to get to me. What kind of a child was I raising? Was he so wrapped up in his own wants that he missed the real meaning of Christmas?

The next day I went through the bookshelf and pulled out a children's Nativity book. When Matthew got home from school, we sat down with J.J. between us and read about the most important birthday in the history of the human race.

When we finished reading the story, I closed the book feeling satisfied that I had reminded Matthew where the true meaning of Christmas really lay: in a manger in Bethlehem, not in outer space action figures and electronic games.

The next afternoon, he was back at the catalogs again.

I lost my temper. "Matthew, didn't we sit down yesterday and read all about Baby Jesus and how He had nothing more than a wooden crib full of hay to sleep on? You're old enough to know that Christmas isn't all Santa Claus and new toys. It's a lot, lot more. Now go upstairs and clean up your room!"

As Christmas approached, I became even more depressed. I knew Matthew had heard what I said, but the impact wasn't there. My child, my Christian child who went to church every Sunday, didn't care about the priorities of Christmas.

The day before Christmas arrived. Early in the afternoon, my ex-husband came, laden with gifts. We had agreed to spend Christmas Eve together for the children's sake. But as soon as Mark walked in the door he announced that the visit would be briefer than expected. "There's a blizzard warning in effect and the tollway is starting to ice up already. I hate to do this, but fifty miles is a long drive in weather like this."

The boys seemed happy with even the small amount of time their father could spend with them. Then Mark left and the cold, cloudy day dripped into evening, Christmas Eve. We dressed for church and I went to make a few phone calls to see who could share the evening with us, now that our plans had been changed. But I hung up the receiver without ever dialing. "Don't be foolish, everyone has plans for Christmas Eve," I said to myself. "We'll just spend the evening together."

During the church service, J.J. fell asleep on my lap and Matthew squirmed in his seat next to me. Afterward we went up to the manger scene with its full-size figures and fragrant hay. Kneeling in front of it,

J.J. still dozing on my shoulder, I heard people greeting one another in cheerful voices. Some were families I knew, but at this moment I felt far apart from them. I gazed at the faces of Mary, Joseph and the Christ Child, thinking, *This is the festival of the Holy Family . . . have we somehow become strangers to them, too?*

In the parking lot, the drizzle had changed to snow. By now, J.J. was awake and crabby from falling asleep at an odd time. He sat in the car whining as Matthew tried to soothe him by telling him it was only a matter of time before Santa delivered the toys.

Santa, Santa!

As I stood, wiping slushy snow off the windshield, the tears wanted to come so bad. But I just wouldn't let them. *Not on Christmas Eve.*

At home, I got the boys ready for bed, and then they climbed into my lap to hear "'Twas the Night Before Christmas," part of our ritual ever since Matthew was born. The words, memorized from so many years of reading, sounded mechanical. The way I felt.

I settled J.J. easily into his crib. In Matthew's room, I found him already under the covers, but wide awake. I kissed him. "Try to fall asleep now." He closed his eyes tightly and I turned off the light.

Downstairs, I made a pot of tea and sat down in front of the fireplace, which was adorned with the empty stockings. There should have been a crèche on the mantel. There should have been so many things about this Christmas.

I looked around the room and tried to find something, anything, that would make me feel the Christmas spirit. My eyes settled on the lighted tree, then on the snow falling on the evergreens outside the front window, making a picture-perfect scene. But it seemed cold and lifeless. I was so lonely.

The tea grew cold. I was just getting up to take the tray into the kitchen and start bringing the gifts from their hiding place when I heard his voice: "Mom?"

I was so startled that I lost my balance and sat back down in the chair.

"I couldn't sleep, Mom."

"Matthew, you *must* go back to bed."

"Mom!"

"Yes, what is it?" I asked.

"I know there isn't any Santa Claus. I know *you're* Santa Claus."

He jumped off the last step and came over to me, climbing onto the chair as he always did, still so easily, still so little boyish. I put my arms around him.

"What makes you think so?"

"Oh, I heard some of the older kids talking. I kind of thought that was the way it was, but I wasn't really sure. I didn't know if I should tell you, so I just went along with it like always."

Suddenly my little eight-year-old had crossed one of the borders of childhood!

"Let's roast some marshmallows," I said abruptly, eagerly. "Want to?"

He nodded. "But first, one thing," he said, turning around to me and getting off my lap. "Can I help you make Christmas for J.J.?"

"Of course," I said.

"Great!" Matthew said, already taking command. "Let's get the crèche for the mantelpiece. J.J.'s got to know for sure that most of all Christmas is Jesus."

It was then I knew Christmas had arrived. And I was the one who'd been worried about all those toy catalogs! How good it felt, suddenly, to be a mother. To know that all the little efforts I'd made to show the boys the real meaning of Christmas hadn't been for nothing.

We walked out into the breezeway that connected the garage to the house and lifted the crèche out of its box.

Overhead, in the holy night, we heard the bells of St. Linus Church begin to ring out "The First Noel," announcing the hour of the ancient, infinite miracle.

—*Jacqueline Ziarko Werth*

Pattern of Love _____

I didn't question Timmy, age nine, or his seven-year-old brother, Billy, about the brown wrapping paper they passed back and forth between them as we visited each store.

Every year at Christmastime, our Service Club takes the children from poor families in our town on a personally conducted shopping tour. I was assigned Timmy and Billy, whose father was out of work. After giving them the allotted four dollars each, we began our trip. At different stores I made suggestions, but always their answer was a solemn shake of the head, no. Finally I asked, "Where would you suggest we look?"

"Could we go to a shoe store, sir?" answered Timmy. "We'd like a pair of shoes for our Daddy so he can go to work."

In the shoe store the clerk asked what the boys wanted. Out came the brown paper. "We want a pair of work shoes to fit this foot," they said.

Billy explained that it was a pattern of their Daddy's foot. They had drawn it while he was asleep in a chair.

The clerk held the paper against a measuring stick, then walked away. Soon, he came with an open box. "Will these do?" he asked.

Timmy and Billy handled the shoes with great eagerness. "How much do they cost?" asked Billy.

Then Timmy saw the price on the box. "They're sixteen ninety-five," he said in dismay. "We only have eight dollars."

I looked at the clerk and he cleared his throat. "That's the regular price," he said, "but they're on sale; three ninety-eight, today only."

Then, with shoes happily in hand, the boys bought gifts for their mother and two little sisters. Not once did they think of themselves.

The day after Christmas the boys' father stopped me on the street. The new shoes were on his feet, gratitude was in his eyes. "I just thank Jesus for people who care," he said.

"And I thank Jesus for your two sons," I replied. "They taught me more about Christmas in one evening than I had learned in a lifetime."

—Jack Smith
as told to Raymond Knowles

The Gift of a Child _____

Christmas comes at different times for me every year. I never know precisely when it will arrive or what will produce its spirit, but I can always be sure that it will happen.

Last year Christmas happened while I was visiting my parents in Conneaut, Ohio. The day was frightfully cold, with swirls of snow in the air, and I was looking out of the living room window of my folks' home, which faces St. Mary's Church. Workmen had just finished constructing the annual Nativity scene in the churchyard when school let out for the day. Children gathered excitedly around the crèche, but they didn't stay long; it was far too cold for lingering.

All the children hurried away—except for a tiny girl of about six. The wind lashed at her bare legs and caused her coat to fly open in the front, but she was oblivious of the weather. All her attention was riveted on the statues before her. Which one I couldn't tell. *Was it Mary? The Baby? The animals?* I wondered.

And then I saw her remove her blue woolen head scarf. The wind quickly knotted her hair into a wild tangle, but she didn't seem to notice that either. She had only one thought. Lovingly, she wrapped her scarf around the statue of Baby Jesus. After she had covered it, she patted the Baby and then kissed it on the cheek. Satisfied, she skipped on down the street, her hair frosted with tiny diamonds of ice.

Christmas had come once again.

—*Mary Ann Matthews*

Davie's Gift _____

Christmas was less than two weeks away, and my divorce decree was one week old. I sat at the kitchen table ostensibly chopping vegetables for stew, actually covering with a homely mechanical task what was a paralysis of mind and spirit.

What am I going to do? I thought over and over. *How can I raise him myself? What should I do?* And as counterpoint to this, *And what about Christmas?*

No job, a slender stipend and a big house I couldn't afford to maintain. And that fine son who deserved so much, for whom I wanted to do so much. *I can't face Christmas,* I thought to myself. And then bitterly, *Face it? I can't even afford it.*

One thing was certain. This year there wouldn't be the problem of the mound of presents spilling over from underneath the tree so that one couldn't get through to the bookcase. There wouldn't be lots of things. I felt guilty because I couldn't provide the things I wanted my son to have.

Davie, my ten-year-old, had chosen to stay indoors this Saturday morning, which was too blustery for kicking the football around on the field back of the house. Instead he had been working alone on some project of his own in that specially designed and equipped workroom on the lower level of the house—that house I could no longer afford. Now he appeared through the door at the top of the stairway. His arms were covered with blue paint to the elbows, he had a smudge of blue paint on his face, and he started talking before he was through the door.

"Mother," he said, "could I have some of that pink stuff you smear on your face?"

I got him the bottle of liquid makeup, he disappeared down the steps, carefully closing the door behind him as per house rules, and I went back to brooding.

One year we spent over thirty dollars just for wrapping paper, I thought. *There was so much of everything . . .*

Davie was back again. "Would we have some white cloth?" he asked hopefully.

"What kind of white cloth?" I asked. "There's a bunch of your old T-shirts in your bottom dresser drawer."

This seemed to fill the bill and he disappeared down the stairs.

Where will I get money for a party? I thought to myself. *And all the Christmas cards to buy, plus the postage, plus . . .*

This time Davie went directly to his own room and I heard him rummaging in his closet. "I need that box of animals I got one year when I was a little kid," he told me, "the cows and sheep and stuff."

All those years of work and sharing, how could it all be swept away . . . ? I went over it and over it hopelessly in my mind, chasing the same question around, when I heard Davie kicking at the door.

"Open the door," he called, "I can't."

When I opened it I saw why. He was carrying his "project," delicately balancing it between outstretched hands.

"I made it for us for Christmas," he said, doing his best to mask pride with good ten-year-old pretense at indifference.

It was a manger. More than a child's manual arts project, it was what I think is artistically called a primitive. It was made from a cardboard carton with one of the two larger sides standing vertical to the rest. This vertical side alone was painted a bright blue. Centered on the blue, covering more than half the surface, was a large silver, and uneven, five-point star.

The wonder of the familiar scene had been captured rather than denied by the crudity of the materials. There on the straw-covered (packing excelsior) floor were the oxen and the lambs with a Mary (a Sears catalog photograph in a hooded robe and mounted to cardboard) brooding on one side of a paper crib. In the crib lay the babe, pink, innocent, incipient, all the promise of the newborn. Only if one leaned over very closely could one see that it was a sewing machine light bulb covered with liquid makeup and wrapped round and round in a scrap of T-shirt.

I had seen many mangers, but never one that at once evoked reverence and a terrible sympathy for the physical hardships of that birth. This is how it must have been in Bethlehem: crude yet full of magic; primitive but flooded with love.

I couldn't tell Davie, as he stood there expectantly waiting for a comment, that in that moment I had learned about Christmas. All day I had fretted about the drab Christmas facing us—no money, no gifts, no parties, none of the material things that had always made Christmas what I thought it was supposed to be.

Now Davie had shown me that Christmas was really about a Child Who brought hope to the world, just as the child standing next to me brought hope to me, teaching me about the joy of creativity and about faith in God's protection—for that is what hope is.

"It's beautiful," I said. "We never had a manger before. We'll put it right in the center of the living room bookcase where everyone can see it."

And as he proudly bore it off I added to myself as much as to him, "After lunch we'll test the tree lights. High time we got ready for Christmas."

—*Ruth E. Stout*

The Star and the Cross
Are Always There

It was Christmas Eve. I stood at the kitchen sink peeling potatoes. A gentle snow was falling, as it should be on Christmas Eve, and I knew I should be counting my blessings. The children had arrived home safely for the holidays. We were cozy and warm. But this was the first Christmas since my husband's death; my loneliness seemed to increase every time I dropped one signature from each Christmas card, selected each gift alone, planned a menu without his favorites.

As I found myself resenting life's cruelties, my son bounced in and silently pushed himself in front of me, jumping up and down, moving his head from side to side, searching the snowy sky.

I knew what he was looking for. In our small town, a cross on the church steeple and a star on the water tower, always lighted during this season, could be seen from our kitchen window. Each year my son eagerly awaited their appearance. Tonight, though, the snow obscured them.

"What's the matter, son?" I asked. "Aren't they there?"

He looked at me in amazement. "Oh, they're always there, Mom," he said, "only sometimes you just can't see them."

Pent-up resentments and self-pity disappeared as I bent to kiss his cheek. How right he was. The star and the cross were waiting for me. A special child had made me see—a very special child, because, you see, in the eyes of the world, my son is mentally retarded.

—Maxine DeGarmo

O Lord, Watch Over _____
These Your Special Children

A gray cheerless morning, two weeks before Christmas in 1981. There we were, thirty-two of us huddled against the chill, waiting for the fast-food restaurant to open. Washington, D.C., had looked beautiful when we arrived the night before, with Christmas trees in every square and streetlights transformed into enchanted towers with twinkling lights and garlands. But now, looking at the cold, unlovely street dotted with X-rated movies and bars, I wished we'd stopped for breakfast in a better section of town.

The group I was shepherding is called The Miracles, a traveling choir from The Baddour Center, in Senatobia, Mississippi. Baddour is a community for mildly retarded adults, and all twenty-five members of the choir were residents there. These special people all hold full-time paying jobs at the Center. Their tasks range from simple to quite complex, depending on their abilities, and their productivity is phenomenal. On weekends The Miracles travel to churches and halls all over Mississippi and neighboring states, giving concerts. In fact, they have sung in twenty-two states and in Mexico. Invariably, audiences come away inspired and with new insights about the gifts and abilities of these "handicapped" adults.

This particular day, we were going to sing in the rotunda of the United States Senate Office Building. Then, after some sightseeing, we'd be off to New York City to give a Christmas concert at Marble Collegiate Church on Fifth Avenue.

There were other people stomping in the cold with us, mostly "street people," or so it seemed to me: men with unshaven chins who carried open bottles wrapped in brown bags, women with bulging shopping bags, and girls in miniskirts and too much makeup.

As the doors opened and we moved into the restaurant's welcome warmth, I noticed one particular girl for the first time. She was young, not more than eighteen or twenty, but she had a hard, frayed-around-the-edges look, as if she had already been used up by the city. She was wearing tight jeans and a short jacket of fake fur. Her arms, when she removed the jacket, were mottled with cold, because her skimpy blouse was for summer wear. Her shoes were backless clogs that *clip-clopped* when she walked. In a pathetic stab at glamour, she had pulled her not-too-clean hair to one side and fixed it with a large white artificial flower. It was obvious that she had been up all night. It seemed just as obvious, to me, why.

"Come on, Miracles," I called, motioning them to a group of tables along one wall. "Let's sit over there!"

Most people might think that traveling with and supervising a group of twenty-five retarded adults would be difficult. Not at all. The Miracles are a wonderful group who listen to instructions, cooperate beautifully and maintain a happy, positive attitude. But ordering breakfast for The Miracles is not quite so easy. At last, however, I got the list straight—I think: twenty-two orange juices, sixteen milks, fourteen orders of pancakes, fourteen coffees, seven Egg McMuffins and five scrambled eggs with sausage. And after one or two spilled coffees and juices, we settled down to eat.

As usual, we got our share of stares from other people, and I knew it wasn't because we were all dressed alike in our spiffy new red blazers with the Baddour insignia on the breast pockets. No, people always stare, because they see The Miracles are "different."

I was heading back for the last of our coffees when the girl with the fake fur reached out and touched my arm. "Hey . . . who are you all?"

I looked into her tired eyes, red-rimmed and caked with too much mascara. "We're called The Miracles," I replied and I explained that we were on tour and were headed for New York City. The girl meanwhile was twisting a cigarette in her fingers. "That's real nice," she replied, looking at The Miracles with unabashed curiosity.

I came back with the coffee and sat down with Ruth, our bus driver's wife.

"What was that all about?" Ruth asked, looking at the girl with as much curiosity as the girl had looked at our group.

"She just wanted to know who we are," I replied, buttering my pancakes. I was just in the act of raising my fork to my mouth when I looked again at the girl sitting at an empty table. Not even a coffee cup . . . and she looked hungry . . .

I put my fork down. On impulse I went to the counter and asked for another order of pancakes, sausages and coffee. "How about having breakfast with The Miracles?" I said to the girl as casually as I could, putting the tray in front of her. She was flustered, unsure of how to react, and then, even without my saying anything to them, The Miracles began drifting over toward her.

Richard and Thornton, Nancy and Audrey, Jeanna and David—they all brought their trays and sat down near her. Soon all of them were talking animatedly, forks waving, the girl laughing. "Can you believe that?" I said to Ruth.

Nancy, who's the receptionist at Baddour, was giving the girl a Baddour Center Who's Who: "Richard Hollie here doesn't read a note of music," Nancy was saying with pride, "but he's a concert pianist. And this is Thornton Chisom, our lead singer. He's got the greatest voice!"

"You sing?" the girl asked Thornton, puffing on her cigarette. "I always wanted to be a singer." Then she looked off into space and said, "I'm from Texas."

"Are you? So am I!" Thornton exclaimed, beaming.

When we had finished eating, we collected ourselves and started to leave. We were all feeling good, Thornton especially, for as he got to the door, he turned and began singing. "Come On, Ring Those Bells," he sang in his rich baritone. Then the rest of us joined in. The people in the restaurant, at tables, and behind counters, gaped, first in astonishment, then in pleasure. There we were, in our trim red blazers, singing happily away, and, to my great surprise, I saw that the girl had joined the group. There she was, right in the middle of us, this gawky girl in her tight jeans and sloppy clogs, trying to sing along and grin at the same time.

We finished our song, and the restaurant burst into applause and cheers. A grizzled old man croaked, "Merry Christmas to all!" waving his brown paper bag.

Jeanna, who has Down's syndrome, turned to the girl and said, "You come and see us at Baddour. Okay?"

"I will! I will!" the girl said happily.

"Merry Christmas!" The Miracles called out, pushing through the door into the December air.

On the bus I made the head count. Something was wrong; I checked again. Then I discovered why; there was one too many. The girl had boarded the bus, too.

"Hey, Miracles!" she called out. "Do you know 'Silent Night'?"

"Sure we know that!" I said. But, glancing out of the bus windows,

I saw that the morning rush hour traffic was already clogging the street. We would have to move the bus. *Well, the cars can just wait a minute!* I told myself as I raised my hands.

"Si-a-lent night, ho-o-ly night . . ." the sweet voices sang in unison. The last notes of the beloved old carol died away, amid the sounds of honking horns and motors.

"Thank you, Miracles . . . thank you!" the girl said almost in a whisper as she got off the bus. She ran quickly to the center island of the busy street, then turned and waved. We all crowded to the windows, waving back until the bus turned the corner.

As we drove to the Senate Office Building for our concert, I looked around. The Miracles—Jeanna, Audrey, Richard, Thornton, Douglas, Nancy and the others—were chattering away, looking at the store windows and the streets beginning to crowd with holiday shoppers. By now The Miracles had forgotten the girl, but I couldn't get the picture of her out of my mind—standing there on that traffic island, smiling and waving.

The Miracles had touched her, I knew that, touched her with their friendliness, their innocence, touched her because they too were different. And for just a moment my mind's eye saw this girl who wanted to be a singer going home again, home for Christmas to some little town in Texas where she could begin to live and dream again.

Lord, I prayed in my heart, as the bus crawled through traffic, *please watch over this Your child, whoever she is, wherever she goes. Watch over her as You've watched over these Your special children who have their own special gifts to give.*

The bus lurched to a stop. Looking through the window I saw the letters carved on the building: Offices of the Senate of the United States.

"Okay, Miracles!" I called. "We're here. Everybody out!"

—*Sybil Roberts Canon*

Trouble at the Inn

For years now whenever Christmas pageants are talked about in a certain little town in the Midwest, someone is sure to mention the name of Wallace Purling. Wally's performance in one annual production of the Nativity play has slipped into the realm of legend. But the old-timers who were in the audience that night never tire of recalling exactly what happened.

Wally was nine that year and in the second grade, though he should have been in the fourth. Most people in town knew that he had difficulty in keeping up. He was big and clumsy, slow in movement and mind. Still, Wally was well liked by the other children in his class, all of whom were smaller than he, though the boys had trouble hiding their irritation when Wally would ask to play ball with them or any game, for that matter, in which winning was important.

Most often they'd find a way to keep him out, but Wally would hang around anyway—not sulking, just hoping. He was always a helpful boy, a willing and smiling one, and the natural protector, paradoxically, of the underdog. If the older boys chased the younger ones away, it would always be Wally who'd say, "Can't they stay? They're no bother."

Wally fancied the idea of being a shepherd with a flute in the Christmas pageant that year, but the play's director, Miss Lumbard, assigned him to a more important role. After all, she reasoned, the Innkeeper did not have too many lines, and Wally's size would make his refusal of lodging to Joseph more forceful.

And so it happened that the usual large, partisan audience gathered for the town's yearly extravaganza of crooks and crèches, of beards, crowns, halos and a whole stage full of squeaky voices. No one on stage or off was more caught up in the magic of the night than Wallace Purling. They said later that he stood in the wings and watched the performance with such fascination that from time to time Miss Lumbard had to make sure he didn't wander onstage before his cue.

Then the time came when Joseph appeared, slowly, tenderly guiding Mary to the door of the inn. Joseph knocked hard on the wooden door set into the painted backdrop. Wally the Innkeeper was there, waiting.

"What do you want?" Wally said, swinging the door open with a brusque gesture.

"We seek lodging."

"Seek it elsewhere." Wally looked straight ahead but spoke vigorously. "The inn is filled."

"Sir, we have asked everywhere in vain. We have traveled far and are very weary."

"There is no room in this inn for you." Wally looked properly stern.

"Please, good innkeeper, this is my wife, Mary. She is heavy with child and needs a place to rest. Surely you must have some small corner for her. She is so tired."

Now, for the first time, the Innkeeper relaxed his stiff stance and looked down at Mary. With that, there was a long pause, long enough to make the audience a bit tense with embarrassment.

"No! Begone!" the prompter whispered from the wings.

"No!" Wally repeated automatically. "Begone!"

Joseph sadly placed his arm around Mary and Mary laid her head upon her husband's shoulder and the two of them started to move away. The Innkeeper did not return inside his inn, however. Wally stood there in the doorway, watching the forlorn couple. His mouth was open, his brow creased with concern, his eyes filling unmistakably with tears.

And suddenly this Christmas pageant became different from all others.

"Don't go, Joseph," Wally called out. "Bring Mary back." And Wallace Purling's face grew into a bright smile. "You can have *my* room."

Some people in town thought that the pageant had been ruined. Yet there were others—many, many others—who considered it the most Christmas of all Christmas pageants they had ever seen.

—*Dina Donohue*

Gold, Circumstance and Mud—

Gifts of the Wise Children

It was the week before Christmas. I was baby-sitting with our four older children while my wife took the baby for his checkup. (Baby-sitting to me means reading the paper while the kids mess up the house.)

Only that day I wasn't reading. I was fuming. On every page of the paper, as I flicked angrily through them, gifts glittered and reindeer pranced, and I was told that there were only six more days in which to rush out and buy what I couldn't afford and nobody needed. *What,* I asked myself indignantly, *did the glitter and the rush have to do with the birth of Christ?*

There was a knock on the door of the study where I had barricaded myself. Then Nancy's voice, "Daddy, we have a play to put on. Do you want to see it?"

I didn't. But I had fatherly responsibilities so I followed her into the living room. Right away I knew it was a Christmas play for at the foot of the piano stool was a lighted flashlight wrapped in swaddling clothes lying in a shoe box.

Rex (age six) came in wearing my bathrobe and carrying a mop handle. He sat on the stool, looked at the flashlight. Nancy (ten) draped a sheet over her head, stood behind Rex and began, "I'm Mary and this boy is Joseph. Usually in this play Joseph stands up and Mary sits down. But Mary sitting down is taller than Joseph standing up so we thought it looked better this way."

Enter Trudy (four) at a full run. She never has learned to walk. There were pillowcases over her arms. She spread them wide and said only, "I'm an angel."

Then came Anne (eight). I knew right away she represented a wise man. In the first place she moved like she was riding a camel (she had on her mother's high heels). And she was bedecked with all the jewelry available. On a pillow she carried three items, undoubtedly gold, frankincense, and myrrh.

She undulated across the room, bowed to the flashlight, to Mary, to Joseph, to the angel, and to me and then announced, "I am all three wise men. I bring precious gifts: gold, circumstance, and mud."

That was all. The play was over. I didn't laugh. I prayed. How near the truth Anne was! We come at Christmas burdened down with gold—with the showy gift and the tinselly tree. Under the circumstances we can do no other, circumstances of our time and place and custom. And it seems a bit like mud when we think of it.

But I looked at the shining faces of my children, as their audience of one applauded them, and remembered that a Child showed us how these things can be transformed. I remembered that this Child came into a material world and in so doing eternally blessed the material. He accepted the circumstances, imperfect and frustrating, into which He was born, and thereby infused them with the divine. And as for mud—to you and me it may be something to sweep off the rug, but to all children it is something to build with.

Children see so surely through the tinsel and the habit and the earthly, to the love which, in them all, strains for expression.

—*Rex Knowles*

Christmas— As Mysterious as Ever

Phyllis wasn't an easy child to love. I wanted the best for her and I prayed for God to bless her, but sometimes I did wish she wasn't in the particular Sunday school class I taught. Phyllis had stringy hair, dirty fingernails and a runny nose. She kept apart from the rest of the children and she walked with a sort of stomp. Besides that, she never sat still, she hated to be touched, and she *always* had to have the last word.

I was twenty years old, and that year I supervised my first Christmas program at the big old stone church, Tabernacle Baptist, on

Chicago's West Side. Early in Advent I held the typed pages of the Nativity script in my hand as I stood before the assembled children.

"If you'd like a speaking part in the program, raise your hand," I said, and almost every hand shot up. Not Phyllis's, of course. When everyone who wanted a part had one, I still had a few left.

"Phyllis," I said, "wouldn't you like just a few words to say in the program?"

"Who said I was coming to your program?" she asked, arms folded across her chest and chair tipped precariously on its back legs. "I'm probably going to a party that night," she said grandly.

Lord, I prayed silently, *please help me love Phyllis.*

"Well, I do have a few more parts if you change your mind."

"I won't," Phyllis said, and she didn't.

On dress rehearsal afternoon the children sat in the darkened front pews of the church, whispering to each other as the adults put final touches on the bath towel headdresses of the shepherds and the tinsel halos of the angels.

"Okay, take your places," I called from the back of the sanctuary. The reader began: "In those days, there went out a decree . . ." A shiver rippled over me. Again I was immersed in the age-old story.

"Mary doesn't act like she's gonna have a baby," muttered a husky little voice behind me. Phyllis might not have any desire to be in the program, but she wouldn't miss the rehearsal!

"Shhhh!" I whispered, reaching back to pat Phyllis's hand. She jerked it away, saying, "Okay! Okay!"

In the last scene, only a spotlight shone on the holy family, and the children hummed "Silent Night." It was beautiful—but who was that moving in front of the manger? Phyllis! You never knew where that child was going to pop up next. Now she stuck her hand into the manger, squeezed the doll's arm, and disappeared back into the shadows.

"Phyllis," I called, "what are you doing up there?"

"I'm just looking," she said. "Besides it's not a baby. It's just a doll. I felt it."

Lord, please help me love Phyllis.

"All right," I said to the cast. "Everyone be here at six-thirty so that you'll be in costume and ready to start promptly at seven. See you tonight."

Phyllis stomped up the aisle with the rest of the departing children. *With any luck at all,* I thought, *she will have had enough this afternoon and won't be back tonight.* I knew this wasn't a Christian reaction but I did want the program to go smoothly.

By 6:45 the air was bristling with excitement backstage. Angels helped drape each other's bedsheet robes. Joseph and the wise men adjusted the beard wires that hooked over their ears. Mary stared into the mirror trying to capture just the right look for the mother of the Savior. I moved from group to group, helping where I could. There was no Phyllis to be seen and I began to relax.

Just a minute before seven, Mrs. Wright entered. In her arms she held her tiny new baby. All wrapped in white, he would replace the doll we'd used in rehearsals. "He's just been fed," she said, "so he should sleep during the program."

"You can put him in the manger just as the lights go down," I whispered.

As the organ chimed the beginning of the service, I took my prompter's seat in the front pew. With the opening strains of "Watchman, Tell Us of the Night," the lights came up on the manger scene, and the narrator began.

But instead of the familiar shiver as I heard the beginning of the Christmas Scripture, I felt something bump my knee and give a little shove. "Move over," muttered an all-too-familiar voice. "I decided not to go to the party."

Not taking my eyes from the drama unfolding up front, I moved over and reached out to pat Phyllis's knee. She flung my hand back into my lap.

I'm trying, Lord, I thought.

The angels sang to the shepherds. The shepherds went to Bethlehem and took a lamb for the baby. The wise men went to see Herod and then to the stable. And Mary sat there "pondering these things in her heart." It was lovely. Phyllis sat beside me so quietly that I forgot all about her, and when I realized she was gone, it was too late.

She stomped her way right up to the manger, just as she had done during the rehearsal. But this time she stiffened, awe-struck, then turned, eyes wide with wonder, and came hurrying back to me.

"He's alive!" she said to me in a penetrating whisper.

Across the aisle, someone asked, "What did she say?"

"She said, 'He's alive!' "

Like ripples in a pond, the word passed from pew to pew, all the way to the back of the sanctuary. "He's alive . . . alive . . . alive." The air grew electric as one by one the people in the congregation felt the living presence of the Baby in Bethlehem.

Here was the real reason we all were celebrating. He's alive! Emmanuel—God with us, God incarnate. A tough, unruly little girl had brought the majestic Christmas message home. *God is alive!*

The lights came up, and when we stood to sing "Joy to the World! the Lord Is Come," the sound rocked our big old church as never before.

I put my arm around Phyllis's tight little shoulders. "You were the best part of the program," I said into her ear, drawing her close to my side.

"I wasn't *in* your program," she said. But she didn't push me away.

—*Doris Swehla*

Would You?

"Would you like to hold the baby?"
The gentle Mary might have said
To the shepherds who were kneeling
By her Holy Infant's bed.

"Would you like to hold the baby?"
She might have asked those men of old,
Three wise men who had offered Him
Myrrh, frankincense and gold.

"Would you like to hold the baby?"
She might ask of us today.
"Hold the blessed Christmas spirit
Deep within your hearts to stay?"

—*Ruth Somers*

The joy
of Christmas
memories

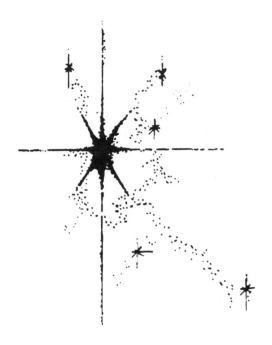

A Christmas Garden

LORD,
In a season of deadness,
When the earth is locked in cold
And the winds sweep through skeleton trees,
We cherish those deep greens and blood reds
Of fir and holly
Standing stark
Against the barrenness of earth
And the whiteness of snow,
Because in the depth of their colors,
We are reminded
That You came to make it
A season of joy.

—*Van Varner*

Sincerely . . . ————————————

It is late Christmas Eve. The fire has burned to embers, the children are asleep. My husband is assembling a doll stroller. I hand him a screwdriver and as I lean back on the carpet my eyes light on a tiny blue and silver rocking horse on the Christmas tree. The ornament is a remnant of my childhood. And as I stare at it, memories wander out of the past . . .

I am a child and it is nearly Christmas. I stand on a kitchen chair pummeling cookie dough with a rolling pin. I wallop the bag of flour right off the counter and it explodes in a cloud of white dust. I do not move, waiting for Mama to explode too. But she doesn't. "What's your favorite cookie shape?" she asks calmly. I find my voice. "A star." Smiling, she hands me the tin cutter. "Make lots of stars while I clean up," she says.

My daddy lifts me onto the seat of his old farm truck and carries me deep into the cold woods to find a Christmas tree. I tramp by a dozen or more that he points out. On and on. I finally choose one, and he says, "Yes, ma'am, I believe this was worth waiting for." He chops it down, loads it onto his big shoulders, and holds my hand all the way back to the truck.

I am sitting in the darkness of my childhood home, gazing at the little tree . . . at a blue and silver rocking horse near the top. Mama calls me to the window and points out a star, big and Bethlehem-bright. We lean on the sill and remember the holy night in a silence that is deeper and richer than any words I have ever heard . . .

The door in time closes as quietly as it opened and I'm an adult again, staring at the ornament and thinking how precious memories are. They live in our hearts and minds, waiting to whisper back to us. Sometimes they come in difficult times, giving strength and hope. Or they come simply to touch us with affection.

Now all at once it occurs to me that perhaps those memories most likely to whisper back do not fall happenstance into our lives. Instead they are *created*. They are handmade by those who have the imagination—and patience—to turn bits and pieces of time into something beautiful for others. It doesn't take much. A pan of cookie stars in a warm kitchen. Holding hands in the woods.

Sandy has finished the doll stroller; a new doll is tucked inside. Silence, now, beside the tree. Then the rustle of a small nightgown at the door. "Oh, Mama!" cries Ann, spying the stroller through the sleep in her eyes. She hugs the doll. I blink at her. Now what? She has spoiled the surprise. But above us the blue and silver horse glistens.

"Want to carry your new doll to bed?" I ask suddenly.

She nods. They will wake up on Christmas morning already friends. But more special still, perhaps on a Christmas Eve yet to come, she too will remember . . .

—*Sue Monk Kidd*

The Christmas I Remember Best

It should have been the worst, the bleakest of Christmases. It turned out to be the loveliest of all my life.

I was nine years old, one of seven children, and we lived in a little farming town in Utah. It had been a tragic year for all of us. But we still had our father, and that made all the difference.

Every year in our town a Christmas Eve Social was held at the church. How well I remember Dad buttoning our coats, placing us all on our long, homemade sleigh and pulling us to the church about a mile away. It was snowing. How cold and good it felt on our faces. We held tight to one another, and above the crunch of snow beneath Dad's feet we could hear him softly whistling "Silent Night."

Mama had died that previous summer. She had been confined to bed for three years, so Dad had assumed all mother and father responsibilities. I remember him standing me on a stool by our big round kitchen table and teaching me to mix bread. But my main task was being Mama's hands and feet until that day in June, her own birthday, when she died. Two months later came the big fire. Our barn, sheds, haystacks and livestock were destroyed. It was a calamity, but Dad stood between us and the disaster. We weren't even aware of how poor we were. We had no money at all.

I don't remember much about the Christmas Eve Social. I just remember Dad pulling us there and pulling us back. Later, in the front room around our potbellied stove, he served us warm milk and bread. Our Christmas tree, topped by a little worn cardboard angel, had been brought from the nearby hills. Strings of our home-grown popcorn made it the most beautiful tree I had ever seen—or smelled.

After supper Dad made all seven of us sit in a half circle by the tree. I remember I wore a long flannel nightgown. He sat on the floor facing us and told us that he was ready to give us our Christmas gift. We waited, puzzled because we thought Christmas presents were for Christmas morning. Dad looked at our expectant faces. "Long ago," he said, "on a night like this, some poor shepherds were watching their sheep on a lonely hillside. When all of a sudden . . ."

His quiet voice went on and on, telling the story of the Christ Child in his own simple words, and I'll never forget how love and gratitude seemed to fill the room. There was light from the oil lamp and warmth from the stove, but somehow it was more than that. We felt Mama's presence. We learned that loving someone was far more important than having something. We were filled with peace and happiness and joy.

When the story was ended Dad had us all kneel for a family prayer. Then he said, "Try to remember, when everything else seems to be lost, the greatest thing of all remains: God's love for us. That's what Christmas means. That's the gift that can never be taken away."

The next morning we found that Dad had whittled little presents for each of us and hung them on the tree, dolls for the girls, whistles for the boys. But he was right: He had given us our real gift the night before.

All this happened long ago, but to this day it all comes back to me whenever I hear "Silent Night" or feel snowflakes on my face, or—best of all—when I get an occasional glimpse of Christ shining in my ninety-year-old father's face.

—Rheuama West

Christmas Is a _____ Time for Imagination

In 1944 my mother and I were two of the sixty-four women that the Nazis held prisoner in a small stable in Ludenburg, Germany. The other women were Jews and we were the only Christians; yet, as Christmas approached, Mother and I felt we had to do something to celebrate the holiday.

"We're going to have a Christmas tree," Mother announced to me suddenly on Advent Sunday. Then she outlined her plan, a plan that would have to be carried out in secret.

On Christmas Eve the other women watched with fascination as we produced a strange collection of treasures and began to "make" a Christmas tree. First there was a long pole that I had found in the barn and had kept hidden under my bed. To this we tied the small pine branches snipped from scraggly trees once destined for the wood pile. An empty tin can, laboriously cut apart and shaped, became our "Star of Bethlehem."

For decorations we made bows out of oddments of colored yarn and festoons cut, kindergarten-style, from scraps of paper. Often, after air raids, we had found long silvery threads on the ground. These now served to wrap our tree in gossamer. At last, after each item had been tied on and in place, we felt that there was still something missing.

"Candles," Mother said. "If only we had some candles."

And immediately it came to me where I could find some—the three lanterns in the pig sty. I crept into the Pig's Villa (we called it that because the accommodations were better than ours) and sliced off a good, but not too noticeable, chunk from each candle.

Now our tree came alive. Its light danced in the eyes of all the women who crowded around it as Mother took out her precious New Testament and read aloud the message of good cheer. Then, softly we began to sing the old carols, ending with *"Stille Nacht, Heilige Nacht."*

Suddenly the door swung open and in strode Max Wagner, a prison officer.

"What is this?" he demanded roughly.

"It is Christmas Eve," said Mother mildly. "We are celebrating the Holy Evening."

"You Jews?" he asked, incredulously.

"My daughter and I are Christians."

"You're no different. You have Jewish blood."

"So did the first Christians," Mother replied firmly. "Christianity is a matter of faith, not race."

Furious, Wagner grabbed our tree, tore it apart and threw the remains in a corner. Then he stomped out, shutting off the lights.

Later, in the darkness, I stretched out my hand to my Mother's hand searching from the bunk below. "We had our Christmas," she whispered.

That evening, we knew for a certainty that Christmas, no matter how or with what it is celebrated, is eternal. But that particular Christmas was made unforgettable by a tree created out of our imagination.

—*Comtesse M. de le Riviere*

A Long Way Home

Every year on Christmas Eve our family comes together to decorate our tree. One by one we hang the familiar ornaments on its deep-green branches, and when the tree is full and resplendent, we stop and wait, in silence. We watch while my husband, Rudy, unwraps the last decoration: an old, much-used paraffin emergency candle. Carefully Rudy reaches up and secures the burnt-down stub to the top of the tree. A match is struck, the wick takes to the flame and at last our family is ready to celebrate another Christmas.

Another Christmas . . . While that squat candle burns briefly, I think of how little it resembles the slender tapers that flickered on the Christmas trees of my childhood in Riga, Latvia. I think of our last Christmas there in 1943, a year of uncertainty. World War II was raging. We Latvians had been caught in the middle of a bloody tug-of-war, first by the Soviet army, then the German, and what lay ahead we could not know.

Even so, my tall, sandy-haired Rudy and our little daughter, Alina, gathered around the tree at my parents' house. Small red apples dangled merrily among the ornaments, and a hand-painted porcelain angel sat serenely on top. The hand-twisted candles of red, yellow, green and white gave a glow to the room as my mother read the Christmas story. We held hands as we sang "Silent Night."

"Look, Alina," said Mother to our tiny three-year-old with blond curls and curious eyes, "these candles remind us that Jesus brings light into our lives just as He brought light into the world. His hand is on us always."

Alina's eyes grew wide. She toddled straight to the tree, took a glass ornament in her small hand—and pulled as hard as she could. We had to run to keep the tree from falling, and the candles from burning the house down!

Another Christmas . . . In 1944 the tide of the war had turned and Russian artillery once again approached Riga. Though most civilians were evacuated from the city so they'd be safe from the shellings, we were not allowed to leave, for Rudy was a much-needed electrical engineer. At last, however, on October 1, Rudy, Alina and I crowded onto a train, the final one to leave. Twelve days later the city fell to the Soviets.

Where did the train take us? To safety? No. To Berlin. To more bombs, more shellings. We stayed in a small rooftop apartment whose owner had fled. Each night we slept with our coats and shoes on, ready to run to the shelter as soon as the sound of sirens split the darkness. Berlin was bombed daily, and often three times a night.

That Christmas Eve I found Rudy putting on his heavy coat. Always a strong, quiet man, he now had a look of determination. "Where—?" I started, but he interrupted me.

"It's Christmas Eve," he said. "I'm going to get our tree."

He emptied the few belongings from our suitcase and went out the door. Rudy rode one of the few "underground" trains to the forest on the outskirts of the city, and there he found a tree just big enough to fit into the suitcase. Hours later he returned.

We placed the tree on a tabletop and we had our Christmas. Rudy read the Christmas story aloud from our Bible, and Alina was given her present, a hand-carved squirrel that Rudy had worked on for months. The back legs moved when Alina pulled on the string. In the dimness the three of us held hands and sang "Silent Night." And for a few hours it was—the sirens were stilled.

Another Christmas . . . We never did see our homeland again. Or those we loved. At the end of the war Latvia became a Soviet state. We had nowhere to go, and nowhere were we wanted. We became three of the thousands of European DPs—displaced persons—and as such were sent to a camp deep in the forests of West Germany. The years went by, one long, empty year after the other.

Five Christmas Eves later, 1949, we were still there. Even on that special day, camp routine never varied. As always, I arose at 4:00 A.M. to peel potatoes with the other camp women. This Christmas Rudy and I were expecting another child, and it was getting harder and harder to make my way to the kitchen through the dark of the morning. Our one meal a day was the never-changing menu of soup.

The forest winds were biting as we trudged from supper in the mess hall to the barracks where we shared one room with four other families. Alina was eight years old now. Her long blond braids fell in bright contrast on the gray of her ever-shrinking jacket.

I tried to get into a happy mood for Christmas, but my spirit felt as murky as the frozen slush we walked through in our camp-issued wooden shoes. *Mother always said God's hand is on us, but where is He?* I wondered. *We want another child, but why now, here? Why have four years of prayers for a home gone unanswered?* I prepared to face another dark Christmas.

Yet in our corner of the drafty tin-roofed barracks stood a proud little tree. It was against regulations to have one, but Rudy had sneaked to the forest once more to find it. Other camp men had done the same for their families. There were no decorations on this tree, no candles proclaiming light to the world. But we had our Bible.

As we read again how Jesus had been born in a stable, no less rude than where we were living now, and how soon after His birth the Holy Family was forced to take flight, I realized that we had our own good reasons to be thankful. We had almost no possessions, but compared to others in the camp, we were rich. We had three chipped enamel plates from which to eat our soup; others had to use tin cans. Alina had only one dress, one pair of underwear and one pair of socks, but every night I had time to clean and mend them. Most of all, however, we had one another—and we still had faith and hope. They were enough to make Christmas bright.

Another Christmas . . . Three months after our son, Johnny, was born, we were notified that we had been selected for immigration to America. A congregation in Kansas City, Missouri, was sponsoring one family. They specified a family with small children—and Johnny was the youngest child in the camp. Not only that, but because children under six months of age were considered too frail for the long ocean journey, we were allowed to go quickly to America, on a plane! In October 1950, six years to the day after we'd arrived in Berlin under fire, we left Germany in an unpressurized cargo plane.

The people of Children's Memorial Lutheran Church in Kansas City embraced us. In the midst of a housing shortage, they found us a small room and paid the first month's rent. One member was a foreman at a factory, and he arranged a job for Rudy. On Thanksgiving, however, the foreman and his wife brought us a roast chicken, a pumpkin pie—and bad news: Business was slow and all new workers were laid off.

The next day Rudy came back from the employment office and joined me at our table. "They had an opening for someone to make coffee boxes," he said with a small smile on his lips. "I got the job. It pays sixty-nine cents an hour."

"Coffee boxes?" I asked, puzzled. But I, too, smiled at our good fortune. Soon we learned that Rudy wasn't making coffee boxes; he was making coffins!

Christmas Eve in Kansas City was sunny, the air crisp but not cold. Johnny gurgled in my lap as I sat at the table, carefully counting our savings: one dollar, plus a few nickels and pennies. There was no question what we'd spend it for. This time I wanted to be the one who would bring home the Christmas tree.

The outside door clicked open as Alina bounced in. Her cheeks were flecked with crimson, as much from excitement as from the December chill.

I carefully gathered the coins in my handkerchief and took her offered hand. We left the baby with a friendly neighbor and walked together to the street corner where a sign read, "CHRISTMAS TREES, $1 A FOOT."

The manager of this operation was a middle-aged man in a red cap and short wool jacket. "What can I get you?" he asked, turning from his last customer.

"We'd like the smallest tree you have," I replied.

He dug in the pile and pulled out an evenly grown deep-green spruce about two feet high. I saw sparks catch fire in Alina's eyes.

"How much?" I asked, my fingers playing nervously over those hard-saved coins.

"Two dollars," said the manager.

"You have nothing smaller?"

"No, lady." The man was gruff.

I could see the look of disappointment in Alina's eyes. We turned and started to walk away. But where were we to find another tree?

"Wait a minute," the manager called after us, his voice momentarily losing its edge. He shook out the little spruce and placed it carefully over Alina's shoulder. "Merry Christmas, little girl."

"Thank you, thank you very much," I whispered, and squeezed all the money I had into his hand. We turned again and walked home joyfully, a Christmas melody on our lips.

That night Rudy drilled a small hole in one of the orange crates we used for chairs and slid the stem of the miniature tree into it. There were no presents *under* that tree, but there were presents all around it: a warm room, a family, a home in a nation called America.

In the bottom of my suitcase I found an emergency candle, and Rudy tied it securely to the top of the tree. Alina stood between us, and Johnny sat on my lap as his father read the second chapter of Luke: "And it came to pass in those days, that there went out a decree. . . . Glory to God in the highest, and on earth peace, good will toward men."

To our gathered family, those were not only words, they were our life. Peace—at last to be without fear, to feel safe, to be free. Good will to men—goodness of heart, help, kindness, love. All this we had experienced from the church people, the factory foreman, the Christmas tree man, the neighbors in this new land.

Then, somehow, the light of that small candle illumined all those dark Christmases past. At last I could see God's hidden hand protecting us from bombs in Berlin and working all things together to bring us from exile in the camp. And I have seen it in the years since, as our children have grown up and had children of their own.

Now when they come to our lovely home at Christmas, we have a tall, handsome tree, and we decorate it with shiny trimmings. But each year, as every year, the highlight of Christmas Eve is the moment

Rudy unwraps the burnt-down emergency candle. When it is burning again, I turn to my son just as I did on the evening of our first Christmas in America. "Look, Johnny," I say. "This candle reminds us that Jesus brings light into our lives just as He brought light into the world. His hand is on us always."

—Maria Didrichsons

Once in a Small Village _____

In December, 1944, the 611th Ordnance Batallion, in which I was a young sergeant, arrived at Rouen, France, shortly before the Battle of the Bulge. Our orders were delayed so we—two hundred men and equipment—were sent to camp in the woods.

Until our orders came through, our only food was meager emergency rations. So one day my tent mate, a PFC named Jim Richmond, and I took cigarettes, hard candies and soap and walked through the snowy woods, hoping to trade them for eggs and cheese at some farmhouse along the way.

After several miles we came upon an empty village, completely deserted. Even the street and road signs were gone, probably removed by retreating German soldiers. The one-room store was locked. No one answered our knocks at the doors of the few houses. To rest and get out of the chill wind, we entered the only other building, a church. Right away I spotted a small organ.

When I entered the army, I could play the organ by ear, so various army chaplains had drafted me to play for religious services. From this I had learned more about the instrument. Now I examined the organ.

It was a two-manual harmonium with pedals for pumping air by the organist and a number of stops for instrumental effects. It was well made but had not been used for a long time. The beautiful carving on it was covered with layers of dust; the bellows were torn and closed, the pedals flat on the floor and at least half the keys depressed. I tried it, but no sound could be coaxed from it.

"I think we could fix it if we had the tools and materials," I said. "The villagers will surely come back as soon as they see that the battle isn't going to be fought here. It would be a wonderful surprise for them to find a restored organ."

Jim agreed. "It's nearly Christmas. It would make quite a present for them," he said.

Since we had little to do until orders came through, here was our chance to make up in a small way for the grief and damage the villagers must have endured in the war.

We returned to camp and gathered the tools we'd need—plus some wire, oil, tire patches, used inner tubes, nails, screws and bolts. The next morning we dismantled the organ, starting at the top, and carefully laid out each screw, washer, spring, stop, reed, key and piece of woodwork in order. Neither of us had taken an organ apart before. But as machinists we had been trained to remember parts in their order, so they could be replaced exactly. When it was finally disassembled, parts of the organ lay in rows in the front pews and on the steps to the altar.

We stripped and patched the bellows with the inner tube rubber and the tire patches. We rewired the pedals so they would work the bellows. We oiled and cleaned each key, reed and stop and then carefully put them back in place. We oiled and polished the woodwork and cleaned the metal till the organ gleamed. It was quite a sight. More important, it played very well when I tried it. The lovely tones echoed in the church as the rays of the late afternoon sun came through the stained-glass windows.

I began to play a Hebrew lullaby my mother had sung to me. I glanced at Jim, who stood beside me, then looked quickly away. His face revealed the homesickness neither of us wanted to voice, just as we did not speak of the heavy fighting we sensed ahead.

"Do you know 'Faith of Our Fathers'?" Jim asked.

I played a verse from memory, then drifted into old carols I had learned as a boy from a neighborly Italian family.

As I stopped playing, and the echoes died, the church suddenly seemed very quiet. In that moment we felt very close to the unseen men, women and children who had prayed here in sorrow as well as joy.

We wanted to stay until someone entered the church. We wished we could witness their delight when they found that their organ would play music again. But we had to be back in camp by six o'clock and we barely had time to make it.

When we reached camp, it was bustling. Orders had come through to move to the front. A warm, hearty supper had been prepared for the whole battalion; tents were being knocked down. By 3:00 A.M. we were all on army trucks rumbling out of the camp.

I looked toward the village, but it was too far away to see. To my surprise, however, the dread of battle was tempered by the scene I imagined taking place there sooner or later, the surprise and pleasure the villagers would surely feel. And in the years since, I have wondered many times who first entered the little church and saw the organ, polished and gleaming. Who first tried it, heard its sounds and perhaps ran into the street to call others? Did it seem like a miracle to them?

They would never know that a Jewish sergeant and a Protestant private revived the organ of their Catholic church. Yet I hope the villagers still remember the restored organ as proof that adversity can make brothers of us all. That's the way I remember it.

—Elliott H. Kone

I Remember Three Christmases

So it comes again, this marvelous Christmas season, the time of chimes and carols, of joy and wonder. A time of fond memories, too, when people look back with love and longing to other Christmases.

There are three particular Christmases in my own past that had a special warmth for me. As everyone knows, gold and frankincense and myrrh were the first Christmas offerings. The gifts given to me on those three occasions were invisible, but they were no less real. Each came unexpectedly—and each left me a changed person.

I

Some of my most impressionable boyhood years were spent in Cincinnati. I still remember the huge Christmas tree in Fountain Square—the gleaming decorations, the streets ringing with the sound of carols. Up on East Liberty Street, where we lived, my mother always had a Christmas tree with real candles on it, magical candles which, combined with the fir tree, gave off a foresty aroma, unique and unforgettable.

One Christmas Eve when I was twelve, I was out with my minister father doing some late Christmas shopping. He had me loaded down with packages and I was tired and cross. I was thinking how good it would be to get home when a beggar—a bleary-eyed, unshaven, dirty old man—came up to me, touched my arm with a hand like a claw and asked for money. He was so repulsive that instinctively I recoiled.

Softly my father said, "Norman, it's Christmas Eve. You shouldn't treat a man that way."

I was unrepentant. "Dad," I said, "he's nothing but a bum."

My father stopped. "Maybe he hasn't made much of himself, but he's still a child of God." He then handed me a dollar—a lot of money for those days and for a preacher's income. "I want you to take this and give it to that man," he said. "Speak to him respectfully. Tell him you are giving it to him in Christ's name."

"Oh, Dad," I protested, "I can't do anything like that."

My father's voice was firm. "Go and do as I tell you."

So, reluctant and resisting, I ran after the old man and said, "Excuse me, sir. I give you this money in the name of Christ."

He stared at the dollar bill, then looked at me in utter amazement. A wonderful smile came to his face, a smile so full of life and beauty that I forgot that he was dirty and unshaven. I forgot that he was ragged and old. With a gesture that was almost courtly, he took off his hat. Graciously he said, "And I thank you, young sir, in the name of Christ."

All my irritation, all my annoyance faded away. The street, the houses, everything around me suddenly seemed beautiful because I had been part of a miracle that I have seen many times since—the transformation that comes over people when you think of them as children of God, when you offer them love in the name of a Baby born two thousand years ago in a stable in Bethlehem, a Person Who still lives and walks with us and makes His presence known.

That was my Christmas discovery that year—the gold of human dignity that lies hidden in every living soul, waiting to shine through if only we'll give it a chance.

II

The telephone call to my father came late at night, and from a most unlikely place—a house in the red-light district of the city. The woman who ran the house said that one of the girls who worked there was very ill, perhaps dying. The girl was calling for a minister. Somehow the woman had heard of my father. Would he come?

My father never failed to respond to such an appeal. Quietly he explained to my mother where he was going. Then his eyes fell upon me. "Get your coat, Norman," he said. "I want you to come too."

My mother was aghast. "You don't mean you'd take a fifteen-year-old boy into a place like that!"

My father said, "There's a lot of sin and sadness and despair in human life. Norman can't be shielded from it forever."

We walked through the snowy streets and I remember how the Christmas trees glowed and winked in the darkness. We came to the place, a big old frame house. A woman opened the door and led us to an upstairs room. There, lying in a big brass bed, was a pathetic, doll-like young girl, so white and frail that she seemed like a child, scarcely older than I was.

Before he became a minister, my father had been a physician and he knew the girl was gravely ill. When he sat on the edge of the bed, the girl reached for his hand. She whispered that she had come from a good Christian home and was sorry for the things she had done and the life she had led. She said she knew she was dying and that she was afraid. "I've been so bad," she said. "So bad."

I stood there listening. I didn't know what anybody could do to help her. But my father knew. He put both his big strong hands around her small one. He said, "There is no such thing as a bad girl. There are girls who act badly sometimes, but there are no bad girls—or bad boys either—because God made them and He makes all things good. Do you believe in Jesus?" The girl nodded. He continued, "Then let me hear you say, 'Dear Jesus, forgive me for my sins.' " She repeated those words. "Now," he said, "God loves you, His child who has strayed, and He has forgiven you, and no matter when the time comes, He will take you to your heavenly home."

If I live to be a hundred, I will never forget the feeling of power and glory that came into that room as my father then prayed for that dying girl. There were tears on the faces of the other women standing there, and on my own, too, because everything sordid, everything corrupt was simply swept away. There was beauty in that place of evil. The love born in Bethlehem was revealing itself again on a dark and dismal street in Cincinnati, Ohio, and nothing could withstand it. Nothing.

So that was the gift I received that Christmas, the frankincense knowledge that there is good in all people, even the sad and the forlorn, and that no one need be lost because of past mistakes.

III

It was Christmas Eve in Brooklyn. I was feeling happy because things were going well with my church. As a young bachelor minister I had just had a fine visit with some parishioners and was saying good-bye to them on their porch.

All around us houses were decorated in honor of Christ's birthday. Suddenly a pair of wreaths on the house across the street caught my eye. One had the traditional red bow, bright and gay. But the ribbon on the other was a somber black—the symbol of a death in the family, a funeral wreath.

Something about that unexpected juxtaposition of joy and sorrow made a strange impression on me. I asked my host about it. He said that a young couple with small children lived in the house but he did not know them. They were new in the neighborhood.

I said good night and walked down the street. But before I had gone far, something made me turn back. I did not know those people either. But it was Christmas Eve and if there was joy or suffering to be shared, my calling was to share it.

Hesitantly I went up to the door and rang the bell. A tall young man opened the door. I told him that I was a minister whose church was in the neighborhood. I had seen the wreaths, I said, and wanted to offer my sympathy.

"Come in," he said quietly.

The house seemed very still. In the living room a coal fire was burning. In the center of the room was a small casket. In it was the body of a little girl about six years old. I can see her yet, lying there in a pretty white dress, ironed fresh and clean. Nearby was an empty chair where the young man had been sitting, keeping watch beside the body of his child.

I was so moved that I could barely speak. *What a Christmas Eve!* I thought. Alone in a new neighborhood, no friends or relatives, a crushing loss. The young man seemed to read my thoughts. "It's all right," he said, as if he were reassuring me. "She's with the Lord, you know." His wife, he said, was upstairs with their two smaller children. He took me to meet her.

The young mother was reading to two small boys. She had a lovely face, sad yet serene. And suddenly I knew why this little family had been able to hang two wreaths on the door, one signifying life, the other death. They had been able to do it because they knew it was all one process, all part of God's wonderful and merciful and perfect plan for all of us. They had heard the great promise that underlies Christmas: "Because I live, ye shall live also."* They had heard it and they believed it. That was why they could move forward together with love and dignity, courage and acceptance.

So that was the gift I received that year, the reaffirmation that the myrrh in the Christmas story is not just a reminder of death, but a symbol of the love that triumphs over death.

The young couple asked if they could join my church. They did. We became good friends. Many years have passed since then, but not one has gone by without a Christmas card from some member of that family expressing love and gratitude.

But I am the one who is grateful.

—*Norman Vincent Peale*

*John 14:19.

Trouble at Wallen's Creek ___

It was the first of December in the 1930s, the Big Depression was in full swing and my husband and I were living in the mountains of Virginia. While there was plenty of good food—home-grown and home-preserved—on the table, there was no cash money available. It is hard to believe, after all these years, that we had to "rob" the hens' nests when we needed a little coffee or sugar, then walk to the little country store to trade the eggs for those items. But that's the way it was.

Every Sunday afternoon I walked over a mile to a little frame Methodist church up the valley, where a few of the older folks were trying to have Sunday school for the children and singing for the adults. There was no preacher, no literature and the only study class was taught from the Bible alone. Old man John led the singing. Each Sunday he brought a few ragged songbooks along with his tuning fork. He would select an old hymn, give the fork a ringing blow on the back of a bench and then "raise the tune." I have never heard more enthusiastic singing in any church.

The first Sunday in December I was thinking of the coming Christmas season, which had always meant so much to me. At church, before the singing started, I asked the group who crowded around the one wood-burning stove for warmth. "Aren't we going to have a Christmas tree for the children and some kind of program?"

I got amazed stares from everyone. Finally John said, "You aimin' to bring a tree into the church house? We ain't *never* done that!"

To justify my proposal I began to tell of the trees we had in town churches and the programs where the children recited their pieces. I did a pretty good job, I guess, for the young folks started to back me up and beg for such a "doin's."

Then a mother asked, "What'd we put on a tree? And we ain't got no money for a treat for the kids."

A little boy piped up, "We're making things for our tree at school," a little one-room building in the valley, "an' teacher's gonna' let us take 'em home after school, an' we could bring 'em here for this tree."

I said that I had some ornaments from my home to bring. Then another woman spoke up.

"We got no treat and all the kids would come lookin' for one. Teacher always gives 'em a little poke of candy, but we got no money for candy."

My feathers really fell then and I was ready to call it off when another mother spoke up. "We *can* have a treat! We all raised popcorn, and we all got sorghum, and I used to make larrupin' good popcorn balls if I do say so myself. I could make 'em again if you'll all help me and fetch some popcorn and molasses."

There it was, we had a treat, and so our plans went forward. The men (there were only four who came to church school) promised to cut the tree on Saturday before Christmas and we could decorate it then.

As the days passed, no problems arose. All went as planned, and Saturday afternoon we gathered to trim the tree. The children had even "drawn names," which meant some little homemade gift would be under the tree for each one. We had no lights, for electricity had not as yet come to the mountains. But when we finished, we all were proud of the way our tree looked and were full of Christmas anticipation.

Sunday came cloudy and cold with light snow flurries. I was so excited I could hardly wait to get started to church. This was my idea, my program. I was bringing the first Christmas tree to that little church. I was so busy patting myself on the back for such a noble deed, however, that I forgot the real meaning and purpose of Christmas.

The mountain folk gathered in early. Little crudely wrapped packages went under the tree and the children just stood around and admired it, pointing out the ornaments they had made from colored paper. The treat arrived in a wagon—two great boxes with brown paper covering the contents—and was carried up to the platform behind the tree. We had to keep shooing the children away to keep the treat a surprise.

At last the program got under way. I was almost bursting with pride (in myself, I'm afraid) as the children said their pieces and sang the carols they had learned. I stood near the tree to call out each child's name as his or her time came. It was in the middle of the program that Gus and Lem came stamping in.

I felt my heart lurch when I saw those two big mountain men, rough as grizzly bears. I knew they had a moonshine still back in the hills and that more often than not they were full of their own "white lightning." I knew, too, that they took a perverse delight in bursting into gatherings where they were neither invited nor wanted and where they frightened and bullied people. Just the day before, Old John had been talking about them. "You know them two fellers that got that moonshine still up in the holler, Gus and Lem? Don't you know they went plumb over to Black Lick last month when those folks tried to have an ice cream supper at the school, and they come in drunk, and they busted up the whole doin's!"

In they came now, stamping their feet, acting like the snow outside was a foot deep instead of just a couple of inches. They didn't take off their caps but pushed across a group of young folks sitting on the back bench with much noise and nudging and laughing. My heart sank into my shoes and I saw Old John give me a frightened look.

I called on the next child and all was fairly quiet as she stumbled through her little verse. When she sat down, however, the noise in the back row started again, this time much louder, and the scuffling got rowdy with a few oaths audible to the congregation. I knew the men had been sampling their own moonshine and I was sick with fright at what might be coming next. It was time for the treat to be passed out, but the disturbance was growing by leaps and bounds, the two men pawing and pulling at the girls near them and pestering them with their rude attentions. The situation was almost out of hand and growing worse. For the first time that afternoon I forgot about myself and my smug self-satisfaction and turned to God for help. I felt like inside I was wringing my hands, and I began saying, "What am I going to do? Please, God, help me!"

Then I heard a Voice within me as clearly as if it had been spoken by the woman next to me. "Ask *them* to help you."

Like Peter of old, I bucked God immediately. "Ask those *drunks,* Lord?" But again it came, "Ask them." This time I did not hesitate, but walked back to the men, who were startled enough to stop their aggressive behavior.

"Fellows, we've got a treat for the kids, but the boxes are heavy and we want to make sure it goes around. Would you help me pass it out?"

They looked as if they doubted their ears, then stared at each other when I asked again. They were so taken aback they didn't know how to refuse and meekly followed me up to the boxes of popcorn balls.

From that minute I never doubted that God had actually spoken to me, for although both men reeked of whiskey, they passed out those big candy balls, grinning from ear to ear as they went through the crowd, seeing that not only was no one slighted, but also that little grabbers were told in no uncertain terms they could only have one popcorn ball.

When they got back to me, I thanked them and insisted they have a candy ball themselves. They shuffled and squirmed, but finally took them and munched through the confection with as much gusto as the children. All was peaceful until the last morsel was eaten, and if molasses and popcorn make for sticky fingers and faces, they also made for much happiness.

When Old John led us in our closing prayer I had to peek, and to my delight, I saw the two men remove their caps and stand still, even if they didn't bow their heads.

As we all departed from the church, it was a humble person who walked home through the snowflakes, for I knew that this Christmas would long be remembered in the valley, and it was all God's doing. My words of thanksgiving came out in a whispered, "Happy birthday, dear Savior, happy birthday."

—*Betty Banner*

Bittersweet Christmas

Christmas was the most special holiday of all for my father. The preparations, gift-buying and decorating were no trouble to him—he enjoyed it all.

Mother told me that he introduced me to my first Christmas tree when I was nine days old. It was a small tree, but every ornament, candle and strand of silver tinsel was meticulously hung in place, as only he could do it. When he had finally finished, he took me from my bassinet and held me up to see his handiwork.

Daddy lived long enough to decorate just four more Christmas trees—each one a little larger than the year before.

The year he died—after a short bout with pneumonia—Mother sat down with me for a talk about Christmas. "Madeline," she said gently, "Santa will be leaving gifts for you, but we won't be having a tree and decorations. It's just too much to do this year."

The morning of Christmas Eve arrived with no special arrangements for the next day, other than early mass and dinner at a relative's house. Just before noon the phone rang and Mother answered. After a pause, I heard her say, "That's very kind of you, but I think we'll spend the evening here together. It's the first since . . ." She recovered, thanked the caller again and hung up.

"Who was it?" I asked.

"One of our neighbors," Mother said. "She wanted us to come down this evening. I . . . I can't."

Mother was silent most of the day. Late in the afternoon, she changed her mind. She called our neighbor and told her we'd stop in for a few minutes.

"It's thoughtful of her," Mother said to me, "and we don't want to seem ungrateful."

When we rang the neighbor's doorbell, she kissed us and led us through the foyer. The living room beyond seemed dark with an odd-colored glow. She motioned us forward, and I stepped into the room and caught my breath. There, shining with colored lights and ornaments and gaily wrapped packages, was a magnificent Christmas tree. Seated around it, smiling broadly, were Mrs. Abrams, Mrs. Cohen, Mrs. Blount, Mrs. Dreyfus. "Surprise, surprise!" they chorused.

Today I can close my eyes and bring back that scene at will. Many times it has sustained me when things have gone badly, when I have doubted the human heart. I can still feel the love of those neighbors—those Jewish women who ventured into an unfamiliar tradition so that one little Christian girl without a daddy could have a merry Christmas.

—*Madeline Weatherford*

Christmas Bells

I heard the bells on Christmas Day
Their old familiar carols play,
And wild and sweet the words repeat
Of peace on earth, good will to men!

I thought how, as the day had come,
The belfries of all Christendom
Had rolled along the unbroken song
Of peace on earth, good will to men!

And in despair I bowed my head;
"There is no peace on earth," I said;
"For hate is strong, and mocks the song
Of peace on earth, good will to men."

Then pealed the bells more loud and deep:
"God is not dead, nor doth he sleep!
The wrong shall fail, the right prevail,
With peace on earth, good will to men!"

Till, ringing, singing on its way,
The world revolved from night to day,
A voice, a chime, a chant sublime,
Of peace on earth, good will to men!

—Henry Wadsworth Longfellow

The
first
Christmas

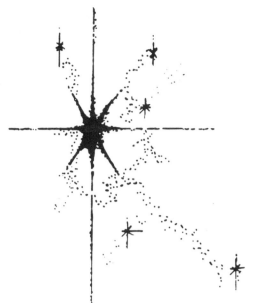

This Quiet Night

Hush,
The Baby sleeps
In the arms of His loving mother.
The night is still
And the beasts of the stable hover
Near in soundless adoration.

Hush,
The world's asleep
In the dreams of this loving Infant.
Our hearts are still
And the beasts of our minds take instant
Calm in boundless adoration.

Sleep, Child, sleep
Your sleep of purity.
Sleep, world, sleep
In God's security.

—*Rehobeth Billings*

The Coming of Christ As Told by Luke

And in the sixth month the angel Gabriel was sent from God unto a city of Galilee, named Nazareth, to a virgin espoused to a man whose name was Joseph, of the house of David; and the virgin's name was Mary. And the angel came in unto her, and said, Hail, thou that art highly favoured, the Lord is with thee: blessed art thou among women. And when she saw him, she was troubled at his saying, and cast in her mind what manner of salutation this should be. And the angel said unto her, Fear not, Mary: for thou hast found favour with God. And, behold, thou shalt conceive in thy womb, and bring forth a son, and shalt call his name Jesus. He shall be great, and shall be called the Son of the Highest: and the Lord God shall give unto him the throne of his father David: And he shall reign over the house of Jacob for ever; and of his kingdom there shall be no end.

Then said Mary unto the angel, How shall this be, seeing I know not a man? And the angel answered and said unto her, The Holy Ghost shall come upon thee, and the power of the Highest shall overshadow thee: therefore also that holy thing which shall be born of thee shall be called the Son of God. And, behold, thy cousin Elisabeth, she hath also conceived a son in her old age: and this is the sixth month with her, who was called barren. For with God nothing shall be impossible. And Mary said, Behold the handmaid of the Lord; be it unto me according to thy word. And the angel departed from her.

And Mary arose in those days, and went into the hill country with haste, into a city of Juda; and entered into the house of Zacharias, and saluted Elisabeth. And it came to pass, that, when Elisabeth heard the salutation of Mary, the babe leaped in her womb; and Elisabeth was filled with the Holy Ghost: and she spake out with a loud voice, and said, Blessed art thou among women, and blessed is the fruit of thy womb. And whence is this to me, that the mother of my Lord should come to me? For, lo, as soon as the voice of thy salutation sounded in mine ears, the babe leaped in my womb for joy. And blessed is she that believed: for there shall be a performance of those things which were told her from the Lord.

And Mary said, My soul doth magnify the Lord, and my spirit hath rejoiced in God my Saviour. For he hath regarded the low estate of his handmaiden: for, behold, from henceforth all generations shall call me blessed. For he that is mighty hath done to me great things; and holy is his name. And his mercy is on them that fear him from generation to generation. He hath shewed strength with his arm; he hath scattered the proud in the imagination of their hearts. He hath put down the mighty from their seats, and exalted them of low degree. He hath filled the hungry with good things; and the rich he hath sent empty away. He hath holpen his servant Israel, in remembrance of his mercy; as he spake to our fathers, to Abraham, and to his seed for ever. And Mary abode with her about three months, and returned to her own house. . . .

And it came to pass in those days, that there went out a decree from Caesar Augustus, that all the world should be taxed. (And this taxing was first made when Cyrenius was governor of Syria.) And all went to be taxed, every one into his own city. And Joseph also went up from Galilee, out of the city of Nazareth, into Judaea, unto the city of David, which is called Bethlehem; (because he was of the house and lineage of David:) to be taxed with Mary his espoused wife, being great with child. And so it was, that, while they were there, the days were accomplished that she should be delivered. And she brought forth her firstborn son, and wrapped him in swaddling clothes, and laid him in a manger; because there was no room for them in the inn.

And there were in the same country shepherds abiding in the field, keeping watch over their flock by night. And, lo, the angel of the Lord came upon them, and the glory of the Lord shone round about them: and they were sore afraid. And the angel said unto them, Fear not: for, behold, I bring you good tidings of great joy, which shall be to all people. For unto you is born this day in the city of David a Saviour, which is Christ the Lord. And this shall be a sign unto you; Ye shall find the babe wrapped in swaddling clothes, lying in a manger. And suddenly there was with the angel a multitude of the heavenly host praising God, and saying, Glory to God in the highest, and on earth peace, good will toward men.

And it came to pass, as the angels were gone away from them into heaven, the shepherds said one to another, Let us now go even unto Bethlehem, and see this thing which is come to pass, which the Lord hath made known unto us. And they came with haste, and found Mary, and Joseph, and the babe lying in a manger. And when they had seen it, they made known abroad the saying which was told them concerning this child. And all they that heard it wondered at those things which were told them by the shepherds. But Mary kept all these things, and pondered them in her heart. And the shepherds returned, glorifying and praising God for all the things that they had heard and seen, as it was told unto them.

—*Luke 1:26–56; 2:1–20*

Mary's Meditations ————

Experience the wondrous events surrounding the birth of the Christ Child as seen through the eyes of Mary, His mother.

Mary's Wonder

The sky of Nazareth burns with a low orange light. I step along under the sunset, following the little shining path, careful not to stumble. After all, I am expecting a child soon. But I could not resist coming once more to the place where the mystery began. I settle on a rock by the spring and watch the sun's low rays sparkle in the water. I remember as though it were yesterday . . .

I had come with my water skins that day, hurrying ahead of the sinking sun. I, a peasant girl moving in the predictable regularities of life. The same spring. The same chore. The same routine. But somehow that day found me full of heightened awareness, alive to God and the world and the possibilities hidden all around me. I was like a child, full of wonder and expectation.

The spring was deserted. I stood there alone for a moment, alert to the presence of God in the rushing water. I dipped my water skin into the stream.

"Mary." The voice broke into the silence. I looked up. No one was about. Only a slanting shaft of sunlight.

"Mary!" The voice poured forth from the streaming light. I froze, my hands steeped in the waters of the cold spring. Slowly I lifted my eyes.

He stood only a few feet away, surrounded by the light. "Do not be afraid, Mary," he said. "I am sent from God. You will conceive in your womb and bear a son. You shall call him Jesus."

"How can that be?" I whispered. "I have no husband."

"The Holy Spirit will come upon you, and the power of the Most High will overshadow you. Therefore the child to be born will be called holy."

Silence hung like a white mist around us. Slowly the words arose from my heart. "Let it be," I said. And the stranger was gone.

The memory fades. Yet even now as I sit by the spring, I feel the wonder of that time. And think of how strange it is that God breaks through to us in the midst of small, common moments . . . how strange it is that every ordinary moment of existence is poised on the brink of a miracle.

And I wonder. If on that day my eyes and ears had been closed . . . if my sense of awe and expectancy had been asleep . . . if my sensitivity to God's coming had been dim . . . would I have heard the angel's voice? And even too, long ago, would my forefather Moses have seen the bush burning in the wind had he not been alert to God's Presence? The spring gurgles and the question looms large in the gentle, falling light.

No, I think. God comes. The extraordinary occurs. And common bushes burn. And there are those who are aware.

Mary's Promise

The stigma follows me like a shadow in the Nazareth street. And although I fight them, tears sting my eyes. For even now after all these months, the women whisper when I pass. And the scandal grows thick with gossip. "There goes Mary. She sinned before her wedding and now she blasphemes God by claiming that her child is conceived from the Holy Spirit. Does she think we are mad to believe such a lie?"

I glance back at the whispering women. Their eyes stare at me with raw accusation, piercing my heart. *Dear Joseph, at least you believe me,*

I think as I hurry into the courtyard of our house. I drop my market basket with sudden weariness. The long months of rejection and hurt wash over me in great black waves. "O God, what have You asked of me?" I cry.

The air is quiet except for the sound of Joseph's hammer thudding rhythmically in his carpenter's shop behind the house. His voice, too, drifts out in faint song, the cadence weaving through the pounding of the hammer. In those quick, decisive blows I seem to hear my own words as they answered the angel. "Let it be . . . let it be." I had freely accepted the extraordinary proposal of God. Yet, how can I go through with it? What good will come of it?

I sit down beside the gate. Joseph's hammer pounds and pounds. His song grows louder. He is singing one of the ancient psalms of King David. "Sing praise to the Lord. . . . Weeping may endure for a night. But joy comes in the morning."*

The words suddenly suffuse me with their promise. The promise that all of God's nights are followed by His mornings. The assurance that He brings light out of dark, hope out of hurt, good out of trials.

Joseph's voice dies away now but the promise remains, warm and deep and certain inside of me. The accusing eyes, the stigma, the tears—they will fade just as the night fades. Joy will arise as God's purpose is fulfilled.

Here by the gate I whisper the words again, "Oh, yes, my Lord. Let it be."

Mary's Calling

The night is well-aged, yet I am sleepless. The tiny unborn one inside moves and thrashes about. *What are you doing, little one? Don't you know the hour?* I stroke my abdomen as though my touch may somehow serve as soothing lullaby. Yet he stirs again, anxious, it seems, to be free of his safe and silent cocoon, eager to take his place in the stream of life.

Oh, it will not be long, little one. Soon you will nestle in my arms. Soon you will romp on the hillsides, chase the fat lambs and toss pebbles into the spring. And too soon you will skin your knees, and

*Psalm 30:4–5, NKJV

later you will taste the pain and heartbreak that await in this world. When that time arrives, I cannot protect you as I do now. I pray that I am ready for the fearful responsibility of being your mother. It seems beyond me now, and I am humbled at the thought.

The night grows older. I lie still now, not daring to shift upon my bed. For at last he is quiet . . . he sleeps. I alone am awake, listening to the distant night sounds, pondering the stillness within me and the life that grows as it was bidden.

Why have I been chosen? How mysterious it is! God could simply speak this child into existence should He wish. Yet we are collaborators, God and I. I smile to myself in the darkness. For to share with God is, I know, the deepest joy of human life. And I know, too, that the joy is given not to me alone. It is a gift to all who would participate as God's partner in the world, transforming His creation into His kingdom.

Outside, the moon glides across the sky too quickly, drawing the night away from us. "Sleep on, little one," I whisper. "Very soon you too will enter upon your high and holy alliance with the Lord."

Mary's Journey

The black and silver sky bends over us like the dome of a shining temple. Far in the East a lone star gleams with a peculiar intensity. I watch it as Joseph adjusts the pack on the donkey.

"We must hurry if we are to be off before day breaks," he says.

It will be a long journey to Bethlehem, where Joseph must pay his tax. Five . . . even six days. We must cross the Jordan and climb the treacherous Judean hills. What I fear most is that my child may be born on the cold, lonely road. My time is so very near.

As Joseph lifts me upon the donkey's back, I cannot ignore the sudden rush of fears. The donkey's hoofs ring hollow on the cobbled street. *Oh, stop!* I want to cry out. *Let me remain here in my safe bed. Here, when I can deliver this child while surrounded by my mother and my aunts.* But Joseph and I plod on, silent shadows in the fading night, moving as though in a dream.

At the edge of Nazareth where the stone street gives way to dirt,

I turn and look back. Somehow I know that nothing will ever be the same again . . . the journey has begun.

I watch Joseph's sure hand tug the little donkey forward into the darkness. I am struck by a simple thought: *Are we not led by God as surely as Joseph leads the donkey?* High up in the clear purple night sky the strangely bright star once more draws my attention. It gleams before us like a map in God's window. Would God send us on a journey without lighting the way with His guidance?

Now the sound of the donkey's hoofs on the road does not seem as lonely, nor does the dark distance seem as ready to swallow us up. *This is not a journey of uncertainty, it is a journey of faith,* I tell myself. How can I fear the unknown when I travel through life with the One Who is always there to place a lamp in the window and gently draw me in the right direction?

Mary's Miracle

"It is finished," I whisper, touching my lips to his tiny ear. "You are born, little Jesus."

In one dark and obscure moment it is done. I lie back in the straw, breathless from pain but also from the strange aura of wonder that has settled so thickly upon our tiny stable.

A clean, black night wind stirs the air. The lantern flickers yellow. Dust dances up like swirling gold. I draw the baby closer, watching Joseph arrange tufts of hay in a cow trough. The silence grows deeper.

I kiss the small face nestled against my cheek. And I count his fingers. One . . . two . . . five. One by one they uncurl as the memory of the angel's voice whispers in my ear, "The child to be born will be called holy." *Holy.* The word echoes. Suddenly my heart is beating hard, the eternal question arising within me as I regard the ten tiny, pearl-like fingers. "Oh, human child, whose fingerprints do you bear? With whose fingerprints do you enter into the human world? *Who are you?*"

Joseph turns as though the question had tapped him on his shoulder. Now all is still in the little stable. The moment seems to hang on the end of a thread, held in suspension by God Himself. And ever so slowly the answer comes, until it bursts into full-blown awareness. This baby—my baby—who stares at me from the depths of his eyes is of us, and yet . . . and yet he is not. He is *Emmanuel. God-With-Us.*

I gaze up at Joseph, my heart and soul too full to speak. And somehow Joseph knows as well. It was there all along—in the prophet's foretelling, hidden in the words of the angel's announcement, quietly in the babe's miraculous conception, in the awed wonder that has clasped the stable. And now the answer is alive in the light that pierces my heart.

I hold little Jesus close against the night, knowing even now that his birth belongs not to me alone. For this baby, so newly born, will be reborn to all generations of people as they too ask the eternal question: *Who are you?* And they will hear the same answer ring out from their hearts.

And so now, here in the shadowed stable where the miracle has arisen like dawn upon the still-sleeping world, I touch my lips to my child's ear once more. "No, my little son," I whisper. "It is not finished. It has only just begun."

Mary's Offering

I awaken suddenly, forgetting for a moment where I am. Brilliant sunlight pours through the doorway, forcing my eyes to close again. Then I remember: I am a mother! I sit up to face the shimmering light. *Jesus? Jesus—my baby—where is he?*

Across the stable Joseph cuddles a small bundle in his arms. "Now, now," he says with a smile. "Didn't I tell you your mother would soon be awake?" He tucks Jesus into the straw beside me. Such a tender little miracle is this child! I kiss the top of his tiny nose, my thoughts floating back to the events of the night just past . . . the silent band of men dressed in shepherds' garb who appeared so soon after his birth, kneeling beside my child. When they departed, they were curiously different men, their voices raised in song and praise to God. Do they know who my baby is?

Now, here in the daylight, the knowledge of his identity arises within me like a fresh new wind, a wind that will gather strength and sweep across all humanity, forever changing its destiny. Beyond the stable walls I hear the sounds of the world as it plods by—Roman horses, wagon wheels, Jewish sandals—moving to the jingle of Caesar's coins, churning the ancient dust through the streets. How strange that the throng should file by in this manner, so close to God's own revelation and yet so unaware.

In the stable a lamb bleats softly and a gentle breeze moves chill shadows through the air. Joseph draws a blanket about us. I trace my finger across the sleeping baby's face. *My precious one, I do not know why you have come. Perhaps the reason has to do with all these people outside who wander past so casually.*

"Oh, Joseph, if only they knew . . . How could they hurry on by?"

Joseph smiles down at me. His face reflects a yearning that has already begun to kindle within my soul—a hope that one day all will discover this stable and leave it in awe and wonderment as did the shepherds.

I reach for Joseph's hand. The truth shines radiant in the air, brighter even than the sunlight: *God is alive in the world!*

Yet I wonder. How will people respond? What will be their thoughts as they depart this stable? In what manner will this child affect the rest of their days?

Deep in the straw Jesus cries. I bend down and lift him up. And suddenly I know that in this very act my question is answered. I will leave this stable forever lifting Him up . . .

This Child is mine, and He belongs to all.

—Sue Monk Kidd

Evaluation

Born in a borrowed cattle shed,
    And buried in another's tomb;
Small wonder our complacency
    Leaves such a One no room!

But castles were as poor as sheds
    Until that Prince was born on earth,
And tombs were mockeries of hope
    Before He changed death into birth!

—*Elinor Lennen*

The light
of Christmas
love

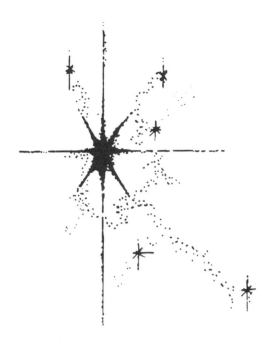

Love Came Down
at Christmas

Love came down at Christmas,
  Love all lovely, Love Divine;
Love was born at Christmas,
  Star and angels gave the sign.

Worship we the Godhead,
  Love Incarnate, Love Divine;
Worship we our Jesus;
  But wherewith for sacred sign?

Love shall be our token,
  Love be yours and love be mine,
Love to God and all men,
  Love for plea and gift and sign.

—*Christina Rossetti*

A Christmas Prayer

Loving Father,

Help us remember the birth of Jesus, that we may share in the song of the angels, the gladness of the shepherds, and the worship of the wise men.

Close the door of hate and open the door of love all over the world.

Let kindness come with every gift and good desires with every greeting.

Deliver us from evil by the blessing which Christ brings, and teach us to be merry with clear hearts.

May the Christmas morning make us happy to be Thy children, and the Christmas evening bring us to our beds with grateful thoughts, forgiving and forgiven, for Jesus' sake. Amen!

—*Robert Louis Stevenson*

The Man Who Missed Christmas

It was Christmas Eve, and, as usual, George Mason was the last to leave the office. He walked over to a massive safe, spun the dials, swung the heavy door open. Making sure the door would not close behind him, he stepped inside.

A square of white cardboard was taped just above the topmost row of strongboxes. On the card a few words were written. George Mason stared at those words, remembering . . .

Exactly one year ago he had entered this selfsame vault. And then, behind his back, slowly, noiselessly, the ponderous door swung shut. He was trapped—entombed in the sudden and terrifying dark.

He hurled himself at the unyielding door, his hoarse cry sounding like an explosion. Through his mind flashed all the stories he had heard of men found suffocated in time-vaults. No time clock controlled this mechanism; the safe would remain locked until it was opened from the outside. Tomorrow morning.

Then the realization hit him. No one would come tomorrow— tomorrow was Christmas.

Once more he flung himself at the door, shouting wildly, until he sank on his knees exhausted. Silence came, high-pitched, singing silence that seemed deafening. More than thirty-six hours would pass before anyone came—thirty-six hours in a steel box three feet wide, eight feet long, seven feet high. Would the oxygen last? Perspiring and breathing heavily, he felt his way around the floor. Then, in the far right-hand corner, just above the floor, he found a small, circular opening. Quickly he thrust his finger into it and felt, faint but unmistakable, a cool current of air.

The tension release was so sudden that he burst into tears. But at last he sat up. Surely he would not have to stay trapped for the full thirty-six hours. Somebody would miss him. But who? He was unmarried and lived alone. The maid who cleaned his apartment was just a servant; he had always treated her as such. He had been invited to spend Christmas Eve with his brother's family, but children got on his nerves, and expected presents.

A friend had asked him to go to a home for elderly people on Christmas Day and play the piano—George Mason was a good musician. But he had made some excuse or other; he had intended to sit at home with a good cigar, listening to some new recordings he was giving himself.

George Mason dug his nails into the palms of his hands until the pain balanced the misery in his mind. Nobody would come and let him out. Nobody, nobody . . .

Miserably the whole of Christmas Day went by, and the succeeding night.

On the morning after Christmas the head clerk came into the office at the usual time, opened the safe, then went on into his private office.

No one saw George Mason stagger out into the corridor, run to the water cooler, and drink great gulps of water. No one paid any attention to him as he left and took a taxi home.

There he shaved, changed his wrinkled clothes, ate breakfast and returned to his office, where his employees greeted him casually.

That day he met several acquaintances and talked to his own brother. Grimly, inexorably, the truth closed in on George Mason. He had vanished from human society during the great festival of brotherhood; no one had missed him at all.

Reluctantly, George Mason began to think about the true meaning of Christmas. Was it possible that he had been blind all these years with selfishness, indifference, pride? Wasn't giving, after all, the essence of Christmas because it marked the time God gave His own Son to the world?

All through the year that followed, with little hesitant deeds of kindness, with small, unnoticed acts of unselfishness, George Mason tried to prepare himself . . .

Now, once more, it was Christmas Eve.

Slowly he backed out of the safe, closed it. He touched its grim steel face lightly, almost affectionately, and left the office.

There he goes now in his black overcoat and hat, the same George Mason as a year ago. Or is it? He walks a few blocks, then flags a taxi, anxious not to be late. His nephews are expecting him to help them trim the tree. Afterwards, he is taking his brother and his sister-in-law to a Christmas play. Why is he so happy? Why does this jostling against others, laden as he is with bundles, exhilarate and delight him?

Perhaps the card has something to do with it, the card he taped inside his office safe last New Year's Day. On the card is written, in George Mason's own hand: *To love people, to be indispensable somewhere, that is the purpose of life. That is the secret of happiness.*

—*J. Edgar Park*

One Starry Night

a cold
and lonely world.
men struggling
to touch
a far-off God.
and then,
one starry midnight
in Bethlehem
God bent down
and gathered up
the world
in a warm,
loving embrace
—Christmas

—Sandy Thompson

A Christmas Reminder

More than fifteen years ago, we received an unusual Christmas card. The message was not at all typical of the holiday greetings, but it probably expresses the real spirit of Christmas better than most cards. Every year since then, the card is pulled from the drawer and posted on the kitchen bulletin board as a reminder. Here is the greeting:

THIS YEAR

. . . Mend a quarrel
. . . Seek out a forgotten friend
. . . Dismiss suspicion and replace it with trust
. . . Write a love letter
. . . Share some treasure
. . . Give a soft answer
. . . Encourage youth
. . . Manifest your loyalty in word and deed
. . . Keep a promise
. . . Find the time
. . . Forego a grudge
. . . Forgive an enemy
. . . Listen
. . . Apologize if you are wrong
. . . Try to understand
. . . Flout envy
. . . Examine your demands on others
. . . Think first of someone else
. . . Appreciate
. . . Be kind, be gentle
. . . Laugh a little
. . . Laugh a little more
. . . Deserve confidence
. . . Take up arms against malice
. . . Decry complacency
. . . Express your gratitude
. . . Welcome a stranger
. . . Gladden the heart of a child
. . . Take pleasure in the beauty of the earth
. . . Speak your love
. . . Speak it again
. . . Speak it still again

—*Ruth A. Ritchie*

In Him Was Life _____

I've always loved the stories of Christ's birth as told by Luke and Matthew. But John's way of telling us about His coming has always excited me. "In the beginning was the Word. . . . And the Word was made flesh, and dwelt among us." "In him was life; and the life was the light of men."*

In Him was life. The words soar. Yet I think there are times when we all feel that the light John talks about barely shines on our own daily lives—when the birth of Jesus seems hardly to have made a mark on the world, much less on our own hearts.

I felt that way one Christmas Eve, one of the rare times that Norman and I were away from home for the holidays. We had been traveling in the Far East, and on Christmas Eve found ourselves alone in London. We ate at a favorite restaurant, but there was no Christmas spirit. Then we set out for a walk in the almost deserted London streets. It was bitter, biting cold. The few people we passed looked as lonely and dejected as I felt.

And then, from far away in the darkness, we heard singing. As we walked along, it grew louder. And louder. We rounded a corner, and there we were in Trafalgar Square. Packed with people as far as we could see! Thousands of them, singing at the top of their lungs. "Joy to the world!" they sang, led by the triumphant brass of a Salvation Army band. "God rest ye merry, gentlemen!" The wind dashed the icy spray of a fountain over the carolers, but their cheer was undiminished. Their faces shone as they sang on and on. "Hark! The herald angels sing, 'Glory to the new-born King.' " On this icy evening, people were transformed. Mystically changed by the spirit of a little Baby born years before in Bethlehem.

Norman and I started to sing too. In an instant my weariness dropped away. In Him there *is* life, Norman and I seemed to be singing into the Christmas air. Precious life. Life that should be lived with vigor and excitement. In Him there *is* life. Glory to the newborn King!

—*Ruth Stafford Peale*

*John 1:1, 14, 4.

Bring Us Together

O GOD,

We go through life so lonely, needing what other people can give us, yet ashamed to show that need.

And other people go through life so lonely, hungering for what it would be such a joy for us to give.

Dear God, please bring us together, the people who need each other, who can help each other and would so enjoy each other.

—*Marjorie Holmes*

A *Song for* Elizabeth

December snow swept across the parking lot of Crescent Manor Convalescent Home. As the youngest nurse on the staff, I sat with the charge nurse at the North Wing station, staring out the double glass doors and waiting for the first wave of evening visitors. At the sound of bedroom slippers flapping against bare heels, I turned to see Elizabeth, one of our patients, striding down the corridor.

"Oh, please," groaned the charge nurse, "not tonight! Not when we're shorthanded already!"

Rounding the corner, Elizabeth jerked the sash of the tired chenille robe tighter around her skinny waist. We hadn't combed her hair for a while, and it made a scraggly halo around her wrinkled face.

"Doop doop," she said, nodding quickly and hurrying on. "Doop doop," she said to the man in the dayroom slumped in front of the TV, a belt holding him in the wheelchair.

The charge nurse turned to me. "Can you get her and settle her down?"

"Shall I go after her or wait till she comes around again?"

"Just wait. I may need you here before she gets back, and she never does any harm. It's just that ridiculous sound she makes. I wonder if she thinks she's saying words!"

A group of visitors swept through the front doors. They came in, scraping feet on the rug, shaking snow from their coats, cleaning their glasses. They clustered around the desk seeking information, and as they did, Elizabeth came striding by again. "Doop doop," she said happily to everyone. I moved out to intercept the purposeful strider.

"Elizabeth," I said, taking the bony elbow, "I need you to do something for me. Come and sit down and I'll tell you about it." I was stalling for time. This wasn't anything we'd learned in training, but I'd think of *something*.

The charge nurse stared at me, and shaking her head, turned her attention to the group of visitors surrounding the desk. Nobody ever got Elizabeth to do anything. We counted it a good day if we could keep her from pacing the halls.

Elizabeth stopped. She looked down into my face with a puzzled frown. "Doop doop," she said.

I led her to a writing table in the dayroom and found a piece of paper and a pencil with a rounded lead.

"Sit down here at the desk, Elizabeth. Write your name for me."

The watery eyes grew cloudy. Deep furrows appeared between her brows. She took the stubby pencil in her gnarled hand and held it over the paper. Again and again she looked down at the paper and up at me questioningly.

"Here. I'll write it first, and then you can copy it, okay?"

In large, clear script, I wrote, "Elizabeth Goode."

"There you are. You stay here and copy that. I'll be right back."

At the edge of the dayroom I turned, half expecting to see her following me, but she sat quietly over the paper, pencil in hand. The only sound now came from the muffled voices of visitors and their ailing loved ones.

"Elizabeth's writing," I told the charge nurse. I could hardly believe it.

"Fantastic," she said calmly. "You'd better not leave her very long. We don't have time to clean pencil marks off the walls tonight." She turned away, avoiding my eyes. "Oh, I almost forgot. Novak and

Sellers both have that rotten flu. They'll be out all week. Looks like you'll be working Christmas Eve." She pulled a metal-backed chart from the file and was suddenly very busy.

I swallowed hard. Until now, I loved my independence, my own little trailer. At twenty-two, I was just out of nurse's training and on my own. But I'd never before spent Christmas Eve away from my parents and my brothers. That wasn't in the picture at all when I moved away from home. I planned to go home for holidays.

Words that wouldn't come past the lump in my throat raced through my head: "They'll go to the candlelight service without me! They'll read the stories, and I won't be there to hear! What kind of Christmas can I have in a little trailer with nothing to decorate but a potted fern? How can it be Christmas if I can't be the first one up to turn on the tree lights? Who'll make the cocoa for the family?"

Tears burned my eyes, but I blinked them back. Nodding slowly, I walked toward the dayroom.

Elizabeth sat at the writing table, staring down at the paper in front of her. Softly I touched my hand to the fragile shoulder, and the old woman looked up with a smile. She handed me the paper. Under my big, bold writing was a wobbly signature.

"Elizabeth Goode," it read.

"Doop doop," said Elizabeth with satisfaction.

Later that night, when all the visitors were gone, and the North Wing was dark and silent, I sat with the charge nurse completing charts.

"Do you suppose I could take Elizabeth out tomorrow?" I asked. In good weather, we often took the patients for walks or rides, but I didn't know about snowy nights. "I'd like to go to the Christmas Eve service, and I think she'd like to go with me."

"Wouldn't she be a problem? What about the doop doop?"

"I think I can explain it to her. You know, nobody else talks during church, so she'd probably be quiet, too. Look how well she did this afternoon when I gave her something to do."

The charge nurse looked thoughtful. "Things would be a lot easier around here if you did take her. Then you could get her ready for bed when you got back. There'll be visitors to help with the others, but nobody has been here for Elizabeth in a long time. I'll ask her doctor for you."

And so it was that a little first-year nurse and a tall, skinny old lady arrived at First Church on Christmas Eve just before the service began. The snow had stopped, and the stars were brilliant in the clear, cold sky.

"Now, Elizabeth," I said, "I don't know how much you can understand, but listen to me. We're going in to sit down with the rest of the people. There'll be music and someone will read. There'll be kids in costumes, too. But we aren't going to say anything. We'll stand up when it's time to sing, and we'll hold the hymnal together."

Elizabeth looked grave. "Doop doop," she said.

O Lord, I hope she understands! I thought. *Suppose she gets up and heads down the aisle wishing everyone a doop doop?*

I wrapped Elizabeth's coat and shawl around her and tucked my arm under hers. Together we entered the candlelit church. Elizabeth's watery old eyes gleamed, and her face crinkled in smiles. But she said nothing.

The choir entered singing. The pastor read from the Gospel of Luke:

"And there were in the same country shepherds . . ."

Costumed children took their places across the front of the church—shepherds and wise men, angels and the holy family. Elizabeth watched, but she said nothing. The congregation rose to sing "Joy to the World." Elizabeth stood holding the hymnal with me, her mouth closed. The lights in the sanctuary dimmed, and two white-robed angels lighted the candelabra. Finally, the organ began the introduction to "Silent Night," and we stood up.

I handed the hymnal to Elizabeth, but the old woman shook her head. A cold dread gathered at the back of my neck. Now what? Was this the moment when she started down the aisle? I looked at the wrinkled face out of the corner of my eye, trying to guess her thoughts. The singing began. I sang as loudly as I could, hoping to attract Elizabeth's attention. As I paused for breath, I heard a thin, cracked voice.

"Sleep in heavenly peace," it sang. "Sleep in heavenly peace."

Elizabeth! Staring straight ahead, candles reflected in her eyes, she was singing the words without a hymnal.

"O Lord, forgive me," I prayed. "Sometimes I forget. Of course it can be Christmas with only a fern to decorate. Of course it can be Christmas without a tree or the family or cocoa. Christmas is the story of love. It's the birth of the Son of God, and it can live in the heart and memory of a gray-haired old woman."

"Christ the Savior is born," sang Elizabeth. "Christ the Savior is born."

"Merry Christmas, Elizabeth," I whispered gently patting her arm.

"Doop doop," she said contentedly.

—*Robin Kurtz*

Prayer

O LORD,

This is a season of light,
    of Bethlehem candles burning.
Help me to bask in that light
    and in that full radiance
    see my brother as he really is.

Help me to sustain that
    recognition of him
As the seasons turn
    and the night sky, once more
Is aburst with the
    brilliance of Your birth.
        Amen.

—*Gordon Neel*

The Woman in A-14 _____

It was the week before Christmas, 1969, in Tegucigalpa, Honduras, my husband's post in the U.S. Foreign Service. It was a busy week, with everyone involved in activities of school, church or club, as well as the preparations for family celebrations in each home.

The U.S. Government Women's Association had planned our annual charitable event, a Christmas party at the *Asilo de Inválidos*— The Old People's Home. As secretary of USGWA, I had the job of calling all the members to remind them to bake cakes and come to help us entertain the patients. More often than not, when I reached a member by phone, she'd say, "I'll be glad to bake a cake, but I don't think I can make it to the party." By the time the last call was made, a little knot of resentment had formed in my stomach.

That's just great! I thought. *Where's their sense of duty, and charity? Some party this will be.* Eight women, out of a possible thirty-five, had said they would be there to help. Eight women, to wait on nearly two hundred patients.

I was reminded of my mother. Mom had died in January of that year; but I knew as surely as I knew anything, that had she been alive and visiting us in Honduras, Mom would have been capable and willing. You could count on her. "If something's worth doing," she must have said a thousand times in my hearing, "it's worth doing right."

We had voted to give the party; now where was the cooperation needed to make it a success? *Well, at least they can count on me,* I thought, nursing my resentment against all those who had refused.

The scowl was still on my face on the day of the party, when I presented myself at the Home to do my share. Gladys, the president of USGWA, was already behind the long table where cakes were being delivered. The Ambassador's wife was there, too, mixing punch and cutting cakes. The handful of women who showed up to help were all occupied with decorating, setting up chairs and doing odd jobs necessary to get the party in motion.

"It's a real shame," I complained to Gladys. "I wish more women were here to help. What do you want me to start on?"

Gladys's warm smile almost melted my bitterness, but not quite.

"Would you mind carrying cake to the patients who can't leave their rooms?" she asked.

"Sure," I replied, grabbing a tray. "I'd better get started. It'll take forever to serve them all."

Music started in the big patio. Someone was leading the patients gathered there in a carol sing. I didn't have time to listen.

Back and forth I ran, toting cake and punch, hardly looking at the patients as I distributed the food and gifts. A small bag with candies and one present was given to each patient in the Home. My legs began to ache from racing up stairs, and the resentment inside me grew with each step. When all were served in one wing, I'd head to another.

On one trip, as I reached the top of the stairs, an elderly lady in a torn, faded print dress reached out timidly and touched my arm. "Excuse me, miss," she whispered. "Could you change my gift, please?"

Irritated, I turned to her. "Change your gift? What's wrong? Did you get something for a man?"

"No . . . no," she stammered. "You see, I got pearls, and pearls mean tears. I don't want any more tears."

What a silly superstition, I thought. *What's the world coming to? You'd think they'd appreciate whatever they get.*

"I'm sorry," I said abruptly. "I'm very busy now. Maybe later." And off I rushed to fill up the tray again, the old woman instantly forgotten.

With a full tray of cake, I hurried to the Women's Ward on the first floor. Backing up to the door of Room A-14, I leaned against it to force it open, turning when I was inside the room. With my first glimpse of the interior of that room I received a shock that started the tray trembling in my hands.

There in the dreary, drab room, on a gray-sheeted cot, and dressed in a threadbare muslin gown, lay *my mother!*

Mom? It couldn't be! Mom was dead; and even if she had been alive, she would never have been in a place like this. This was a home for the homeless, for destitute, aging sick people with no loved ones to care for them. Mom had been ill for six years before her death, but Dad had been there to care for her in her own home, with her children and grandchildren to help and to love her.

No, my eyes were playing tricks on me. I shut them tightly and shook my head. When I opened them again, the emaciated old woman on the bed came clearly into focus. It was not Mom at all! With her straggly gray hair and dull blue eyes, she didn't even resemble my mother. What had ever possessed me to think that poor unfortunate soul was my own flesh and blood?

No, it was someone else, not my mother. Then why didn't I feel relief? The ache swelled inside me, rising to my throat in a huge lump. *I've got to get out of here,* I thought. *I can't let her see me cry.*

Without a word I backed out of the door, just in time. The tears flooded down my cheeks as soon as I was in the dark hallway. Quickly, as if running from some unknown peril, I returned to the cake table where Gladys, still smiling, was cheerfully working. I must have looked as miserable as I felt, for her expression changed to one of alarm.

"Why, Betty, what's the matter?" she asked, putting an arm around me.

"My . . . mother," I sobbed. "I just saw my mother in there. I . . . I can't do this anymore."

"You're just tired, dear," Gladys said. "Take a break."

Others near the table turned to look in my direction. I grabbed a napkin from the table and ran away from the staring faces. I wanted to be alone. But where could I hide? People were everywhere.

Then I spotted the stairs. They were wide and dark, and led down to a landing before turning to continue down to the Men's Ward I'd just finished serving. There was no one on the landing. I headed for it and sank down in the corner, still sobbing.

"Dear Lord," I prayed. "What's wrong with me? Am I losing my mind?"

Almost immediately the answer came, not in audible words, but in the thoughts whirling in my head: *"And though I bestow all my goods to feed the poor . . . and have not love, it profiteth me nothing."**

With a groan I realized that this message was certainly meant for me. Today I had baked cakes, walked miles, carried food, and for what? Whom had I served? Whom had I cared about; or for that matter, had I even bothered to look at? They were all faceless people who meant nothing to me until I saw someone I'd loved in one suffering face. Then they became real.

"I'm sorry," I whispered to the wall. "I've done all of this wrong. I've got to start over again." Taking a deep breath and wiping my eyes,

*1 Corinthians 13:4, ASV

I returned to the cake table. Gladys looked up from her work as I approached.

"You've done enough today, Betty," she said. "Why don't you go on home. We can manage."

"Oh, don't dismiss me now," I answered. "I'm just beginning." I was about to leave with another tray, when the thought hit me. "Gladys, do you have another woman's gift?" I asked. "I must make an exchange."

Gladys handed me a small box containing a small brooch shaped like a heart in bright red stones.

"Thanks, this will be perfect," I told her, taking the box and hurrying toward the patio. Gladys looked bewildered, but I had no time to explain. This new urgency was more important.

Lord, help me to find her, I silently prayed. There was no comfort in knowing that I had not bothered to look at the woman's face. I'd been too busy to care. I'd just "passed by on the other side," and pushed her all too easily out of my thoughts.

I searched the crowd, up one row, down the other. All the faces were bright, smiling, singing carols. The music resounded on my ears. For the first time that day, I began to feel good.

Then I saw the tattered print dress. She was sitting alone against the wall, with her uneaten candy and the pearls in her lap. She looked so sad, so forlorn. I hastened to her side.

"Here you are," I told her. "I've looked all over for you. I brought you a different gift."

She looked up, startled. Then almost apologetically she took the box and opened it. Her eyes lit up like a Christmas tree, and she broke out in a broad grin of delight. "Oh, thank you, miss," she cried. I had to swallow another lump in my throat; but this one I didn't mind.

"Here, let me pin it on you," I said, "and let's get rid of those pearls. We certainly don't need tears for Christmas."

When I left her, she had joined the others, singing carols on the patio. I felt as if a huge weight had been lifted from my shoulders.

There was just one more thing I had to do before the party ended, and that was to return to Room A-14. Somehow I had to thank that patient, and I wasn't quite sure how to do it. But when I pushed open the door, the lady was sitting up in bed eating the cake someone else had brought her. She smiled as I entered.

"Merry Christmas, *Mamacita*" (dear little mother), I said.

"I'm glad you came back," she said. "I wanted to thank you ladies for coming today. I'd like to give you a gift, but I have nothing to give. Could I sing you a song?"

It seems I just couldn't keep that lump out of my throat anymore, so I nodded assent. I sat on the bed while she sang, in a squeaky voice, three verses of the saddest, most non-Christmas song I've ever heard, probably the only song she remembered. But her smiling eyes outshone the lyrics and cemented her message on my heart—Joy to the World!

—Betty Graham

God Bless Us Every One

I have always thought of Christmas time, when it has come round, as a good time; forgiving, charitable time; the only time I know of, in the long calendar of the year, when men and women seem by one consent to open their shut-up hearts freely, and to think of people below them as if they really were fellow passengers to the grave, and not another race of creatures bound on other journeys. . . . And so as Tiny Tim said: "A Merry Christmas to us all, my dears. God bless us, every one."

—*Charles Dickens*

A Christmas Wish

The coal scuttle you see here is only a toy four inches high. It has been in my office for years, but recently I looked at it as though I had never seen it before. It started me thinking about a lot of things, things like old friends and—Christmas.

The scuttle was a gift from a Mrs. Richardson. I recall that my wife and I were sitting with her before a cheerful blaze in the fireplace of her living room one evening years ago. "A fire stimulates thoughts, doesn't it?" I commented.

"Yes," she said. "That's my 'anger fire,' you know." Then she explained how she prayed and meditated beside the fire and it was there that she had learned to face up to the anger she felt for certain people and situations. "I take a lump of coal," she said, motioning to a large black scuttle nearby, "then I place it on the fire and say out loud, 'This is the anger I feel for X.' After that I sit back and watch it go up in smoke."

Several days later Mrs. Richardson sent me the toy scuttle. I was very touched and I was glad, too, to have a way of remembering her story. I put the scuttle on a shelf with other special mementos. And there it sat until recently a visitor asked about it. I had forgotten that it was there.

After the visitor had gone, I looked curiously at the neglected little scuttle. *How like us,* I thought, *with our busy lives, to ignore those objects of special meaning that we have gathered around us for the very purpose of remembering. It's like one of those statues that people pass every day with no idea of the name inscribed on it. But worse,* I thought, *it's like the too familiar possessions in some homes—a family picture, a football trophy, a Bible that is never opened.*

We have to take stock, this scuttle suggested to me, we have to stop and take stock of things—and, yes, of people too—that we take for granted.

And so it is with Christmas.

Christmas is so familiar to us that many of us are unaware of the *real* holiday. Too often we go through the season mechanically: we buy our presents out of obligation; we decorate our homes because everyone does; we see people because we have to. We forget, some of us, that all of the rituals of Christmas have Christ at their center.

And that is how a coal scuttle has brought me to a Christmas wish: that all of us can look with new eyes at the old Christmas meanings and that we can find the familiar beautiful.

—*Norman Vincent Peale*

Many Happy Returns

Many Happy Returns to You, dear Lord.
    May all Your hopes be realized,
May You receive the world's acclaim,
    And its love be undisguised.
May other wise men kneel again
    Bringing gifts of Faith and Love,
And may all lands proclaim You King,
    Blest by the Father's Holy Dove.
And may Your Kingdom enlarge, dear Lord,
    May it steadily increase
Until all the world shall see
    The dawn of Eternal Peace.

—Gladys Allen Cummings

Why Don't We?
—at Christmas

It started years ago as an impromptu little Christmas ceremony in the home of the William T. Clawson family of Monkton, Maryland. The youngest of the three Clawson children, Curt, was in the service then, far away in Korea. At midnight, as the clock ticked away the first seconds of the Lord's birthday, a candle was lighted, a candle so small that it would burn for only eight minutes. While the family gathered around its glow, the father, William Clawson, an advertising executive, read the Christmas story from Luke, and then all the family prayed for Curt and for one another, and for the whole of God's creation. In time those candle-lit eight minutes became an annual ritual, the Clawsons' way of recognizing the truest meaning of Christmas.

More than two decades later the Clawson family tradition was adopted by the Clawson family church, Monkton United Methodist. The small congregation (89 members) of this century-old red brick church asked as many people as it could to join in lighting candles in homes everywhere. They prepared a Christmas card to send out, with a candle enclosed—much like the one the Clawsons had been sending out for years. The card reads:

On Christmas Eve . . .

if everyone lit just one little candle, what a bright world this would be.

if everyone stopped for a few minutes to remember why we celebrate Christmas, what a significant holiday it would be.

if everyone offered just one little prayer for peace on earth, good will to all men, what a more compassionate world this would be.

if everyone started to practice in his own life what he prayed for, what a better world this would be.

at twelve o'clock will you join our family in lighting a little candle, reading the Christmas story from the Bible, saying a little prayer and trying to live a little better?

We hope you will. Also, we hope you have a wonderful holiday season and because of your "practicing," an exciting and enjoyable New Year.

—*The Editors*

A Simple Announcement ___

Each of us has known personal darkness, and many of us have lived through the terrible times when the lights have gone out all over the earth. Yet the longer I live the surer I become that new lights are being kindled. They are little more than sparks, some of them, with quick, tiny glows—but glows of hope as radiant as a nimbus in a shadowy manger.

Last year the Christmas Eve service in our church was more impressive than ever. It is always memorable as we rejoice in song for the gift of a tiny Savior and as each of us there, hundreds of us, lights his or her own candle and holds it aloft until the sanctuary blazes in thrilling brilliance. Last year something was different. It wasn't just that there were extra chairs in the aisles or that the back of the sanctuary was jammed with standing worshipers. As I stood in my pew with flaming candle in hand, I realized that I had seen still another candle lighted, a spiritual candle, one of mutual love and understanding.

Our minister had just made a simple announcement. "This year," he said quietly, "because of the kindness of others, many mothers and fathers of small children are able to be here. They have accepted the thoughtful offer of our Jewish friends at Temple Beth El to take care of the children during this service."

—Ida Hornschuch

Lighting the Way _____

I viewed with apprehension the new homes, apartments and town houses being built in our community. New streets appeared from cornfields and the wooded farmlands gave way to landscaped lawns. New families moved in daily. They came from all walks of life and all parts of the country. I wondered what unifying force could bind us all together.

Late Christmas Eve, as we drove home from church services, I found my answer. In front of home after home, up and down street after street, glowed the light of plain white candles placed in brown paper bags weighted down with sand and set in long, neat rows that curved up to the doorsteps of the houses. Along the edges of snow-covered lawns and around frosty street corners, a myriad of flickering lights shone in the cold dark night. The candles were a modern adaptation of an old religious folk custom—placing small bonfires along the path to church on Christmas Eve to light the way for the Christ Child. My hometown glowed as people united to light the path for the Savior.

A true feeling of joy and peace flooded my heart and the warmth of the candles' glow stayed with me long after Christmas.

—*Marian Parrish*

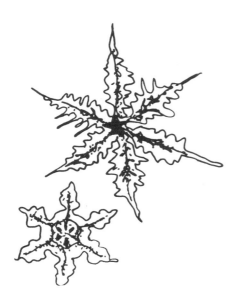

A Christmas Prayer

We open here our treasures and our gifts;
And some of it is gold,
And some is frankincense,
And some is myrrh;
For some has come from plenty,
Some from joy,
And some from deepest sorrow of the soul.
But Thou, O God, dost know the gift is love,
Our pledge of peace, our promise of good will.
Accept the gift and all the life we bring.

—*Herbert H. Hines*

The happiness
of Christmas
sharing

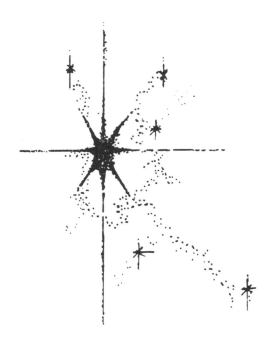

The Message
from the Manger

May the fragrance of the season
  wreathe round your heart today;
May you find a tiny margin
  of time when you can pray.
Let the message from the manger
  bless you, lead you, guide you still;
Join the choir of heavenly angels,
  sing "Peace on earth . . . Good will."

—June Masters Bacher

If We Had Been There

There are some of us . . . who think to ourselves, "If I had only been there! How quick I would have been to help the Baby. I would have washed His linen. How happy I would have been to go with the shepherds to see the Lord lying in the manger!" Yes, we would. We say that because we know how great Christ is, but if we had been there at that time, we would have done no better than the people of Bethlehem. . . . Why don't we do it now? We have Christ in our neighbor.

—*Martin Luther*

Meet Me *in the* City

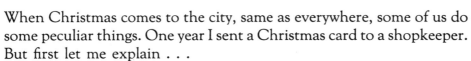

When Christmas comes to the city, same as everywhere, some of us do some peculiar things. One year I sent a Christmas card to a shopkeeper. But first let me explain . . .

You see, New York City is really a large collection of small villages. We reside in tiny territories with boundaries shaped by the shops, churches, schools, cafés and movie houses that we frequent. It doesn't take long to recognize the face behind the counter at the dry cleaner's and the open-til-midnight deli. Soon the news vendor by the subway is saying "Hi," and after a while, the florist throws in an extra stem or two. We're not overly friendly with one another, but I think in our little city-spheres, familiarity breeds *contentment.*

When I lived in another part of the city, however, there was one shopkeeper who was not only unfriendly, he was downright mean. He sold lumber (I was always building bookshelves and things in those days) and he'd cut it to exact sizes. He never looked at me when I'd present my order and any replies were always curt. He'd grunt and grimace and act as if he were doing me a big favor. I didn't like going in there, but his was the only lumber shop in the neighborhood.

To this day I cannot tell you specifically why, but one year as Christmas approached, I sent him a Christmas card. (And something you should know about me—I *never* send Christmas cards.) "Thank you for the good lumber you sold me this year," I wrote on it. Then mailed it and promptly forgot about it.

Months later I needed to go to the lumber loft again. I guess I shouldn't have been surprised—the man was the same. Cold. Not a word was said and again he didn't look at me. I watched him draw a two-by-four from the stacks, cut it and tie the pieces together. Then he took my money and gave me my receipt. I was almost out the door when I heard, "Mr. Varner . . ."

I turned, startled to hear my name. The shopkeeper was standing by his cutting machine. This time he was looking straight at me. At last he spoke.

"Come again," he said softly.

Didn't I say we do peculiar things at Christmas? We seek out relatives who bore us. We spend money we do not have. We send cards to people we don't like. Why? Because we are not ourselves at Christmas. It is one brief time when we become what we want to be, but are too busy or too stingy or too embarrassed to be the rest of the year: sentimental, forgiving, forbearing, generous, overgenerous, thoughtful, appreciative of others.

Jesus came, He said, that we might have life and have it more abundantly. And this is so at Christmas, the anniversary of His birth, when in some beautiful, mysterious way, we live beyond ourselves.

—*Van Varner*

Christmas Is a Time for Remembering

One summer my family gave work to a wandering man even though we suspected he had a problem with alcohol. In the fall he left us, but at Christmas a greeting card arrived from hundreds of miles away—no personal message, just a signature. Then, in the spring, he came to see us.

"I've stopped drinking," he said. "I'm going to a permanent job." When we thanked him for his Christmas card, he told us that it was the only card he had sent. "I wanted it to say 'Thank you,' not for the work, but for the respect you gave me. It helped me to begin a new life."

Then there was the lady in the state hospital. She carried the card a friend of ours sent her in a little drawstring bag and during the entire Christmas season she would stop people and say, "Look at my Christmas card. The lady I worked for sent it to me. I'm not forgotten." We heard later that that card, the only one she received, was the beginning of her recovery.

Today I approach Christmas by recalling those two lone cards. Each represented a new birth at Christmas and both are a reminder to me that Christmas is always a time for remembering.

—*Reamer Kline*

Let Christmas _____
Happen to You

Christmas is a season of joy and laughter when our cup of happiness brims over. Yet increasingly we hear negative remarks about what a burden the holiday season has become.

This indicates that something is wrong somewhere because Christ never meant His birthday to be anything but a glorious event. Christianity is designed for the transmission of power from Jesus Christ to the individual; a Christ-centered Christmas, therefore, should be the year's climactic experience.

Perhaps we need to use more imagination in recapturing this experience in a personal way, like some creative people are doing.

For example, in front of a Texas gasoline station there hung a big sign last December which read: "Merry Christmas and a Happy New Year to all my customers. The $150 that would be spent on your Christmas cards has gone to help the Rev. Bill Harrod bring Christmas cheer to West Dallas."

In another section of the country a church congregation was asked to bring in all the old clothes they could spare for distribution to the needy. One family sent in all new clothes, bought with money diligently saved all year to buy each other Christmas presents.

Such giving surely expresses the true meaning of the birthday of our Lord. We best honor Him when we live the examples He set. An act of mercy that reflects the inspiration He gave us will create a deeper satisfaction and happiness than giving or receiving the most expensive gift.

Ten years ago the daughter of Mr. and Mrs. Carl Hansen of San Bernardino, California, died of cancer. She was seven years old. After time had healed some of their grief the Hansens realized their little daughter had taught them so much about a child's love that they wished to perpetuate what she had given them. They decided that Mr. Hansen would dress as Santa Claus and together they would visit every bedridden child in town who could not see Santa in the stores.

In two years they were so busy each Christmas that the Elks supplied a gift for each child they visited. Mr. Hansen learned magic to entertain the children, then collected amateur entertainers and developed a show for each visit. There were so many homes and hospitals with love-hungry children that the Hansens eventually decided to make their Christmas visiting a year-round project.

The Psalmist says: "I will remember the works of the Lord: surely I will remember thy wonders of old."* The early Christians celebrated Christmas by remembering the works of the Lord and the wonders of old. It was a day for gaiety, but not for excess. There is something blasphemous and pagan about using the birthday of Jesus as an excuse for exaggerated and commercialized giving and heavy drinking. How many people do we all know who make gift-giving a burden because they spend beyond their means? In their effort to keep up with the Joneses many actually go into debt. They would better express the spirit of Christmas if their gift had more understanding in it than money. Here is an example of what I mean:

In Hewlett, Long Island, the Jewish residents formed a congregation, but did not have a temple and met in a store. The membership outgrew the store, and right before the Christmas holiday they started a building drive for a temple. One of their neighbors, a Roman Catholic named Ricky Cardace, turned over his filling station to his Jewish friends on Christmas and New Year's Day. They would operate it, and all the receipts would go into their building fund.

So giving at Christmas can take many forms not measured by dollars. Here are a few simple suggestions for such giving:

A gift you make yourself is more appreciated—something as simple as a fruit cake or a letter opener; a surprise photo of someone's house, babies or pets. A couple we know painted the porch and front door of their parents' house. To the giver it is a labor of love; to the receiver an offering of love.

The members of one family, during a financial crisis, made personally, by hand, all gifts for each other. This particular Christmas was such a joyful one that its plan has been continued ever since.

If you know of a mother who would like to go out to church, or other activities, but cannot afford a baby-sitter, why not give her a gift certificate for a dozen hours of baby-sitting for the year to come?

Send Christmas remembrances to those who would least expect it from you, the people we often encounter but do not really know: the neighbor who nods good morning daily; the people who clean your

*Psalm 77:11.

office or workroom; the officer who directs traffic at your corner. Best of all, the person you've been most annoyed with!

Making it a point to find out more about these people is an enriching experience. Get the thrill of trips to a hospital, orphanage, a jail. Also it is a wonderful Christmas adventure to help the families of such unfortunates.

Often it is left to children to show us the way to a happier Christmas observance. The ninth grade students in Scotch Plains High School in New Jersey decided among themselves to pool all the money they had meant to spend on Christmas gifts for each other, in class and school observances, and give it to those who needed it more. With the advice and help of their local postmistress, they chose the Muscular Dystrophy Fund as the object of their generosity.

In one western public school the sixth graders were told that in many other lands the religious expression of Christmas was its most important element, and gift-giving a minor and more often a separate part of the celebration, generally held on St. Nicholas Day. Since these lively youngsters had always been under the impression that gifts were the ultimate expression of Christmas, they were understandably surprised, and asked:

"How then should we celebrate the holiday?"

Their teacher asked them all to find the answer in the Bible: One boy wrote out this answer from Matthew 25:35, 40:

"I was hungered, and ye gave me meat: I was thirsty, and ye gave me drink. . . . As ye have done it unto one of the least of these my brethren, ye have done it unto me."

That was a good beginning, the teacher told them, and suggested that they find the least of their brethren in their own town. They did, and began to collect their Christmas fund in a big, empty jar.

On Christmas Day there was enough in the jar for Christmas dinners and gifts for two families. And the children themselves took their gifts to both families. On the way back one of the teachers saw a little girl tightly clutching the empty mayonnaise jar that had held the Christmas fund.

"I'm going to put it under my tree at home," she explained all aglow, "to remind me of the loveliest Christmas I've ever had."

Let such a Christlike Christmas happen to you. You'll like it better than any Christmas you ever had.

—Norman Vincent Peale

The Night
of the Blizzard

On the day before Christmas 1966 it snowed. And it kept on snowing. All afternoon the blizzard whirled past my office window at Trinity Episcopal Church in Gulph Mills, Pennsylvania. I had already shoveled snow twice that morning so that the piling drifts wouldn't jam the church doors. It seemed a futile effort, though. Winds blew the snow in ever higher piles, and the road plows could not keep up with the storm.

The phone had been ringing all day with Christmas greetings, and already people were expressing their doubts about getting to church for our candlelight service: "Larry, the roads in our area may not be passable tonight. I'm afraid to risk them. Who knows, though—maybe it will slack off."

But it didn't. As the winter evening closed in, a nagging disappointment followed me around the empty church.

I knew I'd have to think about canceling the service. Once more I stared out at the storm. *Look at that, even a trolley is stalled. Everything's at a standstill.*

It had been a while since I'd heard a snowplow pass, and across the road a one-car trolley of the P & W line stood stranded. I could just barely make out its shape. If those P & W trolleys couldn't get through, what would happen to all the commuters coming home from jobs and last-minute shopping in Philadelphia?

My thoughts turned back to the evening service. In a world gone tinsel-crazy at this time of year, I looked forward to that one hour, late at night, when men, women and children came together to remember the birth of Jesus. That was the heart of Christmas, celebrated in a

church full of people listening to the Nativity story, kneeling in prayer, and singing together "Joy to the World" and other old-time carols.

Yet how often Jesus got lost in the frantic baking and gift-giving, the parties and the shop window glitter that filled the holidays.

The phone rang. It was my wife, Cathy, calling from the rectory.

"Hi," I said. "How's it going over there?"

"The turkey is in the oven—finally," she announced, "and the kids are making cookies." She paused, then whispered, "When are you going to assemble David's fire truck?"

"Oh, after the service tonight," I told her.

"Larry, there must be three feet of snow out there, and the weather forecast is reporting more. How do you expect people to get through all of that!"

"This is what Christmas is about," I replied impatiently, "not turkeys and trucks! I'm going to have that service. Even if just God and I attend."

"Larry, the kids and I will be there, too."

"Thanks," I said, softening.

"Come on over in a few minutes for some coffee and cookies," she invited.

Tramping back to my office from the warmth of the rectory kitchen, I glanced over to the P & W track. "Good grief, that train hasn't moved!" I noted. Stomping snow off my boots, I walked into my office as the phone rang.

"Hi, Larry." It was Ed, our organist. "There's just no way I can get there tonight." He sounded as let down as I felt.

"That's okay, Ed. Everyone else is snowed in too."

"Too bad," he replied.

"Yeah," I agreed. "You and your family have a good Christmas."

Good Christmas! Where was the good in this Christmas?

Going outside to push some more snow away from the front door, I saw the light from the stranded trolley. Were there people on board? Still?

I waded through drifts up to my thighs and squinted against the wind-driven snow. Peering through a window of the trolley, I pushed on the door to find about forty commuters huddled in clusters, deciding what to do. They were just on the verge of leaving the trolley to find refuge nearby; but, most of all, they wanted desperately to get home.

"Most of my kids' gifts are crammed in these bags!"

"My wife has planned the family dinner tonight. She's going to be upset."

"I haven't even begun my family's dinner. I wonder what they're eating."

"I was supposed to pick up my daughter. I hope she got home okay."

"I have a feeling we're going to be stuck here all night."

A teenager tried to doze.

I broke in: "Hey, listen everyone, I'm from the church across the street. Come on over and get warm!"

Relief spread over the passengers' faces as they gathered their belongings and piled out of the trolley, then waded and stomped a path to the church's door.

We got the coffee going down in the recreation room under the sanctuary, and as our guests began thawing out, I phoned Cathy:

"When that turkey is done, Honey, we could use it over at the church. We've got forty hungry passengers from the P & W, and it looks like they'll be here through the night. They can't possibly get home in this storm."

"What? Sure, they can have the turkey. We'll bring the Christmas cookies, too. I'll call the neighbors. See you in a few minutes."

Then passengers began calling home, and I realized what a gap this storm had left in their holiday. Christmas plans had fizzled and I knew there was frustration felt at both ends of those conversations:

"Honey, I know we've never missed a Christmas together . . . I wish I could be there with you and the kids."

"Hi, dear. Everybody get home safe? . . . Yes, I'm okay. . . . You're decorating the tree? Yeah, I know, it's not the same without you, either."

". . . I know. I've got the kids' gifts. We'll just have to wait. . . . No, there's no way any of us can leave here. I miss you all so much. . . . We're in a church. They're taking good care of us here. . . . Now, don't you worry."

"Baby, don't cry. Daddy will be home just as soon as he can. . . . Be sweet. Give Mommy a hug."

One after another, they called to share a few moments with their families, to let them know they were safe. They wanted to be home, but it was obvious they would be spending the night. Travel was unthinkable. Nothing moved outside but the wind and the snow.

A few of our nearest neighbors fought their way over. Back and forth they came, bringing casseroles and salads, some of their own Christmas fixings, along with towels and toothpaste and orange juice and homemade breakfast rolls for the morning.

A neighbor confided: "We'd given up on getting out tonight. Even for the Christmas Eve service. We just assumed it would be canceled. But when we heard about these poor people trapped in the storm, well, we couldn't let them go without."

As people relaxed and as food was passed, spirits warmed, and gradually laughter filled the recreation hall. A party mood began sweeping through the group. One man came back from calling his wife to tell me:

"She doesn't believe I'm actually in a church. She hears all the laughing and thinks I'm at a party! Come on, Larry, and talk to her. You know what she said? 'You're lying! You haven't been in a church in forty years!' "

And then, before I knew it, it was time for the service. I'd almost forgotten it in the hectic scramble of caring for these people. They were in clusters of conversation. A few had stretched out on the six-foot mats used by children attending our church school.

I cleared my throat and interrupted: "There will be a Christmas Eve service in a few minutes. All of you are welcome to come."

The room became silent. People exchanged glances. In the midst of this hesitation, I left for the sanctuary to prepare for the service.

They all looked so comfortable. Would anyone come?

As I stood in the pulpit and turned the pages of the Bible to the Christmas story, Cathy and the kids came in and sat in the front row. Then our next-door neighbors, Vivian and George Whittam, and their son, George, Jr., followed. Vivian sat at the organ and prepared to play. George turned on the tree lights, and their son lit the white candles surrounded by greenery.

A sparse group. Well, time to begin.

Then the door burst open and the trolley passengers came streaming in, smiling and whispering. And suddenly the church seemed almost full. Full of strangers, all brought by the snow to celebrate the birth of Jesus. And what a moving, worshipful time together! I will never forget it.

At 4:00 A.M. Christmas morning, after all of our guests were tucked in with mats and blankets, I finally got around to assembling David's fire truck. As I sat by the tree putting it together, I thought about the strange turns life can take, how some people had been kept away by the storm while others had been driven in by it.

And I thought about some of the remarks after the service. Like the woman who said if she'd managed to make it home, there would have been the family and the food and the gifts, but not Christ. To her, Christmas now meant something more than it had before the storm.

And to think that I had worried about the number of people who would be there to hear the Good News of His birth. I'll never worry again. For Christmas will always happen; it will not be denied. Christmas is greater than any storm—in nature, or in life.

—Lawrence J. Seyler
as told to Sue Philipp

Because of a Baby

"I don't think Christmas is ever going to come," I said, staring moodily out of the window.

"Why, it's only a little over three weeks away," Mother said.

"I don't mean that. I mean it's not going to seem at all like Christmas this year."

We had lived in Southern California for eight months now, and the mild weather gave us no clue as to the season. We had to consult the calendar to remind us that it was the first week of December.

From where I sat I could see lush green lawns instead of grass a winter-kill brown. Rather than maples reaching bare branches against a mottled gray Kansas sky, I saw palm trees with accordion-pleated fronds on a background of cerulean. Inside there were no familiar pots of impatiens rescued from frost to bloom on the windowsills. Instead we looked out on exotic gardens replete with bird of paradise and lily of the Nile.

So much about our life here in San Diego seemed uncomfortably strange to us. Our small utilitarian apartment in the garish pink stuccoed building bore no resemblance to our weather-beaten old frame house back in the flatlands where we had a commodious kitchen and a maze of rooms upstairs and down.

Most disturbing of all was the fact that we didn't really know many people out here. I had a few friends, but I seldom saw them except at school. Back in Kansas we knew everyone in town. Somebody was always popping in our back door with a jar of home-canned piccalilli or a fruitcake made from someone's great-grandmother's recipe.

Here, we were cheek by jowl with the folks in the next apartment, but the only neighbors' names we knew were those printed on the twenty mail slots in the first floor lobby. What's worse, we couldn't match any of those names with the faces we occasionally saw in the hallway.

Like so many others of that time, our family had moved west hoping to find steady employment. My father felt lucky to get a job as a guard at one of the aircraft factories. But even having work that brought in a regular paycheck didn't make up for the feelings of displacement that we were experiencing. We often prefaced our sentences with the words, "When we go back to Kansas . . ."

Of course, it wasn't all bad. Even though the California winter wasn't our idea of what Christmas weather ought to be, it was fun to be able to astound aunts and uncles back in the Middle West when we wrote letters describing the unusual aspects of our life out here. They couldn't imagine our having a picnic in winter, but that's exactly what we were doing on that first Sunday of December 1941.

It wasn't the kind of fried-chicken-and-angel-food-cake picnic we had been accustomed to back home. This Sunday, right after church, we had gone to Old Town for tamales. Those steaming delicacies, wrapped in corn husks, were placed on trays, which we carried outside. We sat to eat at long trestle tables beneath lacy-leafed peppertrees.

We had only just started to eat when someone called out, "Here's another bulletin coming in about Pearl Harbor."

I'd never heard of Pearl Harbor, but then, geography wasn't my best subject in school. It took us a few moments for the awful news to sink in. We left our trays and gathered around a radio. We listened, stunned, as details of the attack were repeated.

Although we had lived for the past months in a city where soldiers and sailors and marines crowded the streets alongside aircraft factory workers, the thought of actually being at war seemed unreal.

That afternoon my father left the apartment for work at the plant, where he was on the swing shift from three until midnight.

Mother and I stayed close to our table radio. That evening we listened to news reports instead of the "Jack Benny Show."

Just before it was time for me to go to bed, there was a faint knock at our apartment door. I went to answer and was surprised to see a small boy staring up at me.

"My mother's sick," he said and reached for my hand.

Mother followed us along the hallway and into a studio apartment. A single unshaded bulb lit the sparsely furnished room. Along one wall were two canvas cots.

A little girl of two, wide-eyed and obviously frightened, sat on one of the cots. The mother of the children lay groaning on the other.

"The baby's too early," the young woman cried out. "Help me, please."

Mother knelt by the cot and talked comfortingly to the moaning woman as I hurried to find a telephone to call an ambulance.

I knocked on five different doors until I found someone who had a telephone. By the time the young woman was taken to the hospital, the occupants of most of the other apartments on our floor had gathered in the hallway to see what was happening.

"Where's her husband?" asked a man whose Oklahoma tones reminded me of those of my uncle who lived in Ponca City.

"She told me that he's stationed aboard a ship at Pearl Harbor," Mother said. "He was supposed to get leave when the baby was born, but I guess today has changed all that. The poor girl doesn't even know if he's alive."

Mother repeated the story of how young Evie Gibson and her two little children had come to San Diego on a bus from Colorado. She had run out of money because her husband's allotment checks had not caught up with her. Probably it was the news about Pearl Harbor and the worry about her husband that had started labor six weeks early.

"Well, we'd best get these two young'uns bedded down," said a neighbor with a soft Kentucky drawl. "We've got room at our place."

The neighbors moved slowly back to their own apartments, but I sensed in all of us a reluctance to leave the crowded hallway. It was as though we had some unfinished business to attend to.

Early the next morning the woman from the apartment across from ours came over with freshly baked breakfast rolls.

"My name is Hallie," she said. "I come from Wymore, Nebraska."

"Come in, Hallie," Mother invited, and she seemed to savor being on a first-name basis with a neighbor. "Sit down and have a cup of coffee."

"Have you heard anything about Evie Gibson?" Hallie asked.

Mother shook her head, but added, "My husband and I are going to the hospital today to let her know that Johnny and Sally are being well cared for. We'll let you know what we find out."

When I got home from school that afternoon, I learned that Evie had given birth to a four-pound baby boy. Mother spread the word to all our neighbors.

"He's cute as a button," Mother said. "But he's so tiny and Evie is so anemic that the doctor is going to keep both of them in the hospital for a couple of weeks."

Papa contacted the Red Cross and learned that Seaman First Class John Gibson was safe and would be told about his new son.

It was Hallie who came up with the idea about the Gibsons' apartment. "If Evie is going to be in the hospital for two weeks, that will give us time to do something about that terrible place she lives in."

"I've got an extra lamp with a shade that would brighten up that room," said Arla Mae of the soft Kentucky drawl.

"The walls need a couple of coats of paint first," said Sam, who had come from Oklahoma looking for work as a carpenter.

"That new baby can't sleep on a cot," said Shirley in her practical Hoosier manner. "I'll bet Cecil and I can find a crib at a secondhand store."

"We have a Boston rocker we don't use much anymore," offered Lucretia.

So it was that almost everyone in that apartment house thought of some way to make a contribution to the project. The Gibson apartment became the center of activity around the clock. Day-shift people painted walls during the evening. Those on the graveyard shift spent their afternoons trimming woodwork. Swingshift workers scraped paint off windows at odd hours in between.

Little by little that horrid room where Mama and I had first seen Evie and her two children began to take on a homey atmosphere. Furnishings seemed to materialize out of thin air. Shortly after Shirley and Cecil bought a secondhand crib, beds appeared for Evie and the children. Then someone moved in a bedside table. The next day a lamp was put on the table. Before long there was a crocheted doily under the lamp and a small ceramic figurine. Even a couple of framed watercolor prints found their way onto the freshly painted walls. Hallie and Mama, Lucretia, Shirley and Arla Mae worked together for days making patchwork comforters for the beds, exchanging a lot of their own family histories as they talked and sewed.

The day Evie and the baby came home from the hospital, Papa bought two Christmas trees. One for us and one for the Gibsons. We showed Johnny and Sally how to string popcorn and cranberries. To this day I can smell the white library paste we smeared on colored construction paper to make the chains that we looped over the dark green branches. Better still, I can remember vividly the sound of laughter as all of us neighbors gathered to admire the baby and leave gifts under the Gibson's tree. We stayed to sing carols, and for the first time since we left Kansas, Papa got out his fiddle and played, while Sam accompanied him on the harmonica.

I wonder how many of us realized what had happened to us because a baby was born. No longer were we strangers in a strange place. In a way, we had all come home. And Christmas had come after all.

—Mary Blair Immel

The Caring Tree

The experiment was simple enough in concept. The First Baptist Church of Stockton, California, would have a seven-foot Christmas tree in the sanctuary, its only decorations the ornaments made by the children in Sunday school. On the back of each ornament there would be the name of a family or individual in need of help. First Baptist families would volunteer to "adopt" one of these needy families for the Christmas season.

This project, known as The Caring Christmas Tree, had been tried the year before by one of the Sunday school classes. Now, during the Christmas season of 1984, the senior pastor, William D. Webber, hoped for the full participation of his seven hundred-member church.

The Community Concerns Committee had set a goal of one hundred ten needy families to be "adopted" by one hundred ten First Baptist families. But, as the project began, a strange problem presented itself. First Baptist is a well-established, solidly middle-class congregation. What sort of needs did families have? And where would one hundred ten needy families be found?

Today, Mark and Valerie Turner, who chaired the committee, say, "We didn't know many people even outside the church whose needs weren't already being met. We were pretty blind to what was going on around greater Stockton."

Metropolitan Stockton has a population of nearly three hundred fifty thousand people. The city sits in California's Central Valley, one of the world's leading agricultural areas, famous for its vegetables and grapes. A ship channel connects the Port of Stockton to San Francisco Bay and makes it a prime shipping center. During the harvest seasons the fields and docks of Stockton teem with activity.

Between harvests, a grimmer story holds true. At these times, thousands of field hands are without work, with seasonal unemployment rates reaching as high as twenty-five percent. The unemployed tend to live in outlying Stockton, beyond the view of First Baptist families. As church members contacted community agencies, they began to see this sadder side of their city. They also quickly saw that they would have no trouble finding one hundred ten needy families.

Calls and cards began to pour in. Mark Turner says, "Often we'd find from five to ten children living with parents, grandparents, dogs and cats—all in a tiny two- or three-room shack. And yet their requests were so small. Parents rarely wanted anything for themselves. One elderly widow requested only house slippers. A man wrote that he hoped only for a supply of distilled water—which he couldn't afford—for his kidney dialysis machine."

Once aware of such poverty, the church members got to work. First, the children made the one hundred ten ornaments listing the needy families, then hung the decorations on the Christmas tree. The ornaments were removed by church families, who noted the need of their "adopted" family and proceeded to fill it.

Some First Baptist families were retired or struggling financially themselves, so these either chose families who needed services instead of things that cost money, or they banded together with other church members. New friendships were formed as the work progressed.

A week before Christmas, the whole church gathered for a dedication service, and gifts were brought forth and placed beneath the Christmas tree. Says Mark Turner, "Nobody imagined there would be so many gifts—all so lovingly wrapped. There were hundreds and hundreds of them, overflowing the whole front of the sanctuary."

The seven days before Christmas were delivery time, with a coordinated team of volunteers fanning out across the Stockton area to distribute this wealth of gifts. But now another aspect of The Caring Christmas Tree became evident. The outreach project was helping families *within* the church in unexpected ways.

There was the family of Regina Williams, for instance. Regina and her fourteen-year-old son, Michael, and four-year-old daughter, Jennifer, had been living in poverty in a Stockton trailer park for longer than they cared to remember. Regina's husband's disability checks were their only source of income. As the Christmas of 1984 drew near, Regina sank into depression. Once again she would be unable to give her children what they wanted.

When The Caring Christmas Tree Project was announced at her church, Regina initially felt further cause for depression. First Baptist was one of the few bright places she knew in the world, and she dearly wanted to be one of its vital members. But since she lived so close to poverty herself, how could she afford to help anyone else?

Happily, Regina ultimately found her role by becoming a member of the delivery team. And one day she was working with John and Leah Lewis when they stopped at a wrong address by mistake, but in doing so they found a family in desperate straits.

"I know, deep inside, that God led us there for a reason," says Regina. "There were twelve children living there with their parents in only two rooms. They had *nothing.* No Christmas tree, no toys, almost no food. It gnawed at me. I went home that night and said to my own family, 'I think God wants us to help them. Let's see what we can do.' "

They did plenty. They searched their own trailer for household items and toys their "adoptees" might need. They mobilized other people in their trailer park and together made expeditions to thrift shops and garage sales. Regina's children persuaded a teacher that the adopted family should become a class project. Even Regina's mother, on welfare herself, pitched in. When all the gifts were finally ready for delivery, they made a small mountain.

"It was eye-opening to realize that so many needs of others could be met out of the relative poverty of our own lives," Regina says. "That poor family was, of course, very happy to receive all those gifts. But you know, I think my family was made just as happy by giving."

No longer did Regina dread that she was failing to give her children a good Christmas, and no longer did her children have to feel that Christmas was mainly a season of unanswered longings. By reaching out, by offering love to others, they brought new love into their own family.

The Williamses were by no means the only First Baptist members to experience a welling up of love within the family. Many other families enjoyed a similar renewal, all going to prove the main message of The Caring Christmas Tree: that church *outreach* projects help families *within* the church.

Actually, the Tree of Caring caused a chain reaction of goodness that benefited the First Baptist church family as a whole. "In November of 1984," Pastor Webber says, "the church had settled into an apathetic rut. It was hard to get anyone excited about anything. Our budget was badly in the red and giving was declining by the week. But The Caring Christmas Tree was a big turning point for us. Our whole church had come together with a miraculous display of generosity, heaped up and running over. And the generosity didn't begin and end with the Christmas Tree. In no time our deficit was gone. Services were better attended. Hymns rang out."

Once again, the message is clear: Families—church families, too—are strengthened within by reaching out.

—*Susan DeVore Williams*

Christmas Eve

The door is on the latch tonight,
    The hearth-fire is aglow,
I seem to hear soft passing feet—
    The Christ child in the snow.

My heart is open wide tonight
    For stranger, kith or kin;
I would not bar a single door
    Where love might enter in.

—Author Unknown

The blessings of Christmas giving

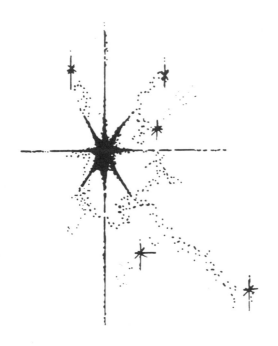

A Prayer for December

HEAVENLY FATHER,
Christmas began
With the gift of Your Son,
Who in turn gave the world
The gift of His life.
Let me remember, O God,
That Christmas remains
A matter of giving,
Not parties, not presents,
Not material wealth,
For Christmas is Christmas
When I give of myself.

—*Van Varner*

The Art of Giving

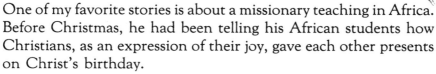

One of my favorite stories is about a missionary teaching in Africa. Before Christmas, he had been telling his African students how Christians, as an expression of their joy, gave each other presents on Christ's birthday.

On Christmas morning, one of the Africans brought the missionary a seashell of lustrous beauty. When asked where he had discovered such an extraordinary shell, the young man said he had walked many miles to a certain bay, the only spot where such shells could be found.

"I think it was wonderful of you to travel so far to get this lovely gift for me," the teacher exclaimed.

His eyes brightening, the African answered, "Long walk, part of gift."

—*Gerald Horton Bath*

"Long Walk"

Nowadays, since our three children are long-married and raising families of their own, Norman and I divide Christmases among them. One year we'll go to Maggie and Paul in Pittsburgh, then another to John and Lydia in Virginia, and the next we'll stay close to home in Pawling, New York, with Liz and John.

We keep up the same traditions in each home—the trimming of the tree, everybody in the house together, no one cooking or reading or doing anything but helping with the ornaments that we take out and exclaim over as if we were suddenly meeting old friends. The tree done, we settle down and Norman reads the Christmas story from Luke, and we sit on the edge of our seats listening as though we'd never heard the story before. Isn't it odd how we all become children again, wanting to hear the same story over and over again? Isn't it odd, and isn't it wonderful!

Sometimes—often—getting to Pittsburgh or Virginia is exhausting work in the Christmas crush of travelers, through wintry skies, and loaded down with festive packages. So is doing all those pre-holiday tasks of arranging our schedules and getting out into the shopping swirl to purchase all those packages we load ourselves up with. Sometimes—often—I'm tempted to throw up my hands and say, "It's too much! It's just not worth the effort." But if Norman is around when I begin to get that feeling of exasperation, he'll give me a wink and say, "Long walk, Ruth, long walk," and I'll laugh and get back to work.

"Long walk" is one of our code signals. Norman and I started using it years ago after reading a little story which appeared in *Guideposts*. The story was about an African boy who presented his missionary teacher with an exquisite seashell as a Christmas gift. The lad had walked many, many miles for it, to a special bay, the only place where such shells could be found.

"I think it was wonderful of you to travel so far to get this lovely gift for me," said the teacher, greatly impressed.

And the boy's eyes brightened as he said, "Long walk, part of gift."

It's true, Christmas is an effort for all of us, but I truly believe that the holiday is made more meaningful, more memorable, *because* of that effort.

Isn't it a part, a valuable part, of our Christmas gift?

—*Ruth Stafford Peale*

My Evergreen Memory _____

The week before Christmas that year had begun as excitingly as all other Christmas weeks I knew in my child's heart—making chains out of colored paper, stringing popcorn, fashioning paste ornaments and trying to be good.

Anticipation swelled and filled the house as the weekend drew near, for on Friday Daddy would come home from his job at the foundry in the city, bringing all the wonderful things of a child's Christmas. There would be toys and dolls and good things to eat. And there would be the happiest gift of all, our Christmas tree, green and full and fresh-smelling, crisp as the winter air, and we would painstakingly adorn it with all the homemade decorations we had created with such expectancy during the week.

Every Friday was long, waiting for Daddy's arrival—but this Friday before Christmas was never-ending. My little brother, Albert, and my nephew Larry, and I sat huddled around the coal stove in the dining room, keeping our toes warm and conjuring up the glorious tree and other, smaller treasures Daddy would soon be bringing. We took turns as lookout at the front door and window, to catch the first glimpse of him.

We pelted Mama with excited questions—how much longer before Daddy came home, how big would the tree be, would it be bigger than last year's, did we have enough decorations? At first she smiled and evaded our questions. But as we grew more eager, more insistent, Mama's round, soft face turned solemn. "I have something I want to tell you," she said softly. "I think it's time you knew."

Daddy, she told us, had telephoned—at our next-door neighbor's because we had no phone—to prepare us for bad news. The foundry had laid him off and there would not be enough money to have our usual Christmas. "We will have to wait and see," Mama said, "but don't be too disappointed if Daddy has no tree when he gets home."

We couldn't believe there would be no tree and when at last the old Dodge pulled into the drive, we tumbled out into the cold night air to greet Daddy and see what he had managed to bring. True to Mama's word of caution, there were few groceries, no presents in sight and, saddest of all, no Christmas tree.

I felt crushed as only a nine-year-old can. There had been Christ-mases in the past when presents were few and sweets carefully doled out. But even in the poorest years we had always had a Christmas tree.

Struggling to hold back tears, I wanted desperately to cry out for someone to give help. But who? We were immigrants in a strange land, Hungarians in a predominantly English community in Canada, Catholics surrounded by Protestants. And we were poor—but so were most of our neighbors.

As I climbed the stairs with Albert and Larry, heading for the room with the big double bed that we three shared, I suddenly began to pray. *Surely God will help us,* I thought. *After all, it is Christmas.* As I prayed, I felt buoyed by my own silent words. I promised Albert and Larry that tomorrow Daddy would find us a Christmas tree.

Saturday dawned cold and bright, with a sparkling blanket of new-fallen snow that cried out to be played in. But Saturday meant chores for us all, with extra duties because it was Christmas Eve. My tasks were to wax and polish the linoleum with a brick encased in a wool sock, gather tinder for the stove, crack walnuts for baking and polish shoes for church on Sunday.

Throughout my chores, I kept sending God my urgent prayers.

Despite Mama's warning and Daddy's empty hands, Albert and Larry and I hung our long brown stockings on our bedpost and wrote our letters listing the toys and other gifts that would make us happy.

Before noon, as he noticed our preparations, Daddy drew us together. He would see what he could do about a Christmas tree for us, he said. But by late afternoon no tree had appeared, and Daddy was still busy in the garage. My prayers grew stronger.

At last Daddy emerged from the garage carrying a two-by-four, about five feet tall, into which he had drilled holes, some on each side. Next, he put on his coat and hat and started up the street.

At the end of our block lived a widow, Mrs. Tinsley. Her property was bordered on three sides by a single row of majestic evergreens, which formed a windbreak to her house. It was Daddy's plan to ask Mrs. Tinsley for some small branches from the bottoms of her trees. Minutes later he returned with the branches, then began inserting them into the holes he had drilled into the two-by-four making our "tree."

Daddy was trying so hard, but by no stretch of the imagination could anyone think of this pitiful device as a real Christmas tree. I didn't want Daddy to see my disappointment, though, so I maneuvered over to the window and pressed my nose to the frosty pane and gazed up at the darkening heavens with tears in my eyes.

As I stood peering at the brightening stars, thoughts of the bright star over Bethlehem came to me, and I suddenly remembered that tomorrow was the Baby Jesus' birthday. I became so engrossed with thoughts of the Baby and the manger and the shepherds on that first night before Christmas that concern about the tree completely left my mind. "Thank You for the Baby Jesus," I whispered. "Thank You for sending Him."

Suddenly I jumped at the sound of a knock at our front door.

Opening it, I found Mrs. Tinsley standing there, a smile on her thin face. Beside her stood her son, home from the service for the holidays. He was grinning, too. In his hands stood the tallest, most beautiful, most perfectly shaped Christmas tree I had ever seen. It was so big and round that it filled the doorway.

By now Albert and Larry were beside me. We were dumbstruck at first. Then shrieks of joy came pouring out of us, making such a commotion that Mama came running from the kitchen to investigate. When she saw us and the tree, she too gave a cry of delight as Daddy and Mrs. Tinsley's son carried the tree into the living room.

While Mama brought out a tray of spiced hot cider and Hungarian *kifli* for our guests, Mrs. Tinsley presented us children with cloth storybooks, candy canes and, especially for me, plaid grosgrain ribbons for my hair.

When our visitors had gone, Albert and Larry and I set about decorating our grand tree with all the ornaments we had made. When we were done, we pronounced it the most wonderful Christmas tree ever. And when the bright sun of Christmas rose, it showed us how even more wonderful our neighbors were, how generous and unselfish their gift. For there in the line of Mrs. Tinsley's magnificent evergreens stood a new, conspicuous, stark and gaping hole. They had sacrificed one of their precious trees to make our Christmas a happy one.

Every day of my growing-up life I saw that gaping hole. It became a poignant reminder of something truly wonderful, so much so that I believe my life was shaped by it.

For though I outgrew my childhood and childhood's desires, my childlike faith has never changed. Though burgeoning branches of other trees now conceal the gap where once "our" tree stood, in my heart I still see it and remember that God hears even the prayer of a child—and answers it with the message that love of neighbor and good will among men are still the glad tidings of Christmas.

—Irene M. Lukas

The Christmas Party _____

It was two weeks before Christmas and I was addressing invitations for a party for my two children, Ann and Mark, and their friends. I should have been looking forward to it, but I wasn't. I had been giving similar Christmas parties for several years and almost every one had been disappointing. My young guests never seemed to feel the magic and the wonder that I remembered from my own childhood.

When I had been a very small girl, our next door neighbor was a retired minister who was a favorite with all the children on the block. Dr. Howard was never too busy to listen to us, to admire our pets and to counsel us in his unobtrusive way. But most endearing of all the things he did for us were his wonderful Christmas parties. Long ago I had made up my mind to duplicate them for my own children, but somehow I never was able to recapture the magic, even though I tried hard to follow the pattern Dr. Howard had used.

The next day I had several errands to do and my route took me through the area where I had spent my childhood. The dingy inner city was all but unrecognizable to me now, and Dr. Howard's stately old home was a travesty of its once-lovely self. But on impulse I pulled in to the curb and gazed at the decaying house. Suddenly, I was eight years old again and approaching that imposing front door.

I remembered how I held tightly to my little brother's hand and how the old-fashioned bell still echoed through the house when Dr. Howard opened the door. He was wearing his clerical black with the wing-collared shirt and bow tie. His white hair curled about his head like a halo, and as always he gave us a radiant smile.

"Dorothy! Bobby! How good of you to come! Wait till you see what a very special surprise I have for you tonight!"

As I greeted the other children, I noted that the Perry boys were as solemn as ever. I supposed this was because their mother had been sick for a long time. The three Donettis were there, too, painfully shy as always because we all knew that their father had gone to prison for embezzlement. The Muller twins in their outgrown clothing were also there. Of course, the two Harris girls were special—I could hardly imagine the bliss of having Dr. Howard for a grandfather!

Movies taken by Dr. Howard in the Holy Land—that was the special treat. Always attracted by faraway places, I was spellbound by the scenes of Jesus' earthly life.

Then it was time for "Going to Jerusalem," the first of a whole series of parlor games. After arranging the chairs, our host took his place at the piano and reviewed the rules: "I am going to play a Christmas carol for you, a favorite of little French children. When the music stops, you must quickly sit down. The winner is the child who gets the last chair."

I loved every moment of Dr. Howard's parties, but the high point for me was always the first sight of the candle-lit dining room and its laden table. Ice cream molded into angels, Christmas trees, wreaths and stars, as well as cake, candy and nuts dazzled my eyes. Never had I seen so many good things to eat.

It all came back to me as I sat there in my car. Then abruptly I was jolted out of my reverie as the front door opened and a careworn woman emerged. *How deprived she looks,* I thought. And then, as I stared at the present-day tenant of Dr. Howard's former home, I had a flash of intuition as shocking as a dash of cold water. Had all the children at those parties been invited because *they* had been deprived in some way? Surely not my brother and myself?

But as I sat there thinking about the past, I was forced to admit that divorce had not been all that common in those days. I could still remember Dr. Howard talking with my separated parents, and my own pain when my father had left. The more I thought about it, the more apparent it became that Dr. Howard's grandchildren had been the only guests who could be said to have come from a "normal" background. As I drove home, it all came into focus. Not only had Dr. Howard given his parties for deprived children, but he had been perceptive enough to recognize differing forms of deprivation.

By the time I had pulled into my driveway I knew exactly what I wanted to do. Going directly to my desk, I picked up the addressed party invitations and threw them all into the wastebasket.

That evening at dinner I talked to my husband, Bob, and the children about my day and its surprising conclusion. At first Ann and Mark were disappointed that their usual friends were not to be invited, but when I had explained that some children needed the invitations more than others, they began to be intrigued.

"Why not ask old Mr. Hughes?" suggested Mark. "He's so cross he never speaks to anyone. A party might give him some Christmas spirit."

"He sure needs it," added Ann. "The kids say he's the meanest man in town."

"That's not very kind, Ann," I said, "and anyway, it's supposed to be a children's party."

"I don't see what difference it makes, Dorothy," my husband said. "Everyone likes a Christmas party."

"Well," I said, "if we're going to include adults, there's Mary Wynn." The middle-aged widow lived on our street, and her continuous and compulsive talking kept most of the neighbors at bay.

Bob suggested two teenagers he had counseled recently at the high school where he taught. Patty had been placed in a foster home and was a most unhappy child. Dan was a chronic disciplinary problem whose divorced mother had washed her hands of him.

Three Vietnamese children who had recently moved to our neighborhood were our last and unanimous choice.

When the night of the party arrived, I nervously awaited our oddly assorted guests, but as it turned out, I needn't have worried. The little Vietnamese charmed everyone with their shy good manners, the garrulous widow melted the stony reserve of "the meanest man in town," and Dan went out of his way to be nice to the nervous and awkward Patty.

I was pleasantly surprised when all the guests, children and adults alike, chose to join in the games and expressed their pleasure in the children's cartoon and the Palestinian travelogue as well. Later, as we gathered around the dining table, faces were glowing. After the carols were over and Mark and Ann produced the simple gifts that had been placed under the tree, the guests' appreciation was so out-of-proportion to the value of the gifts that my eyes burned with tears.

When it was all over, our older guests left to walk home together, wishing us all a "Merry Christmas." Dan and Patty took the Vietnamese tots out to our car, and I was alone in the front hall with my husband, who was pulling on his boots.

"Oh, Bob," I said, "the magic was there this time. I could see it in their eyes—every one of them."

"Giving love to the unloved," he murmured. "Maybe that's more rewarding than just trying to recapture happiness of your own."

"You're right, Bob," I answered as I watched the departing figures waving gaily to each other in the gently falling snow. "It took me a long time to learn that. But Dr. Howard knew it all the time."

—*Dorothy R. Masterson*

Blessings in Disguise _____

Many years ago, when the twentieth century and I were young, my father was pastor of the small Baptist church in Eatonton, the central Georgia birthplace of Joel Chandler Harris, creator of the legendary "Uncle Remus." We loved the town and the people, but Papa's salary of a hundred dollars a month was stretched past the breaking point for our family. We would have found it even harder to get by if Papa's brother Robert hadn't always sent us a five hundred dollar check on the first of December. In fact, all year we looked forward to that extra income.

A small part of that windfall was always allocated for each of us at Christmas, and for weeks we planned what we most wanted to buy with our share.

My seventh Christmas is the one I remember best. Uncle Robert's letter arrived on schedule. In our usual ritual, Mama and we children gathered around Papa's chair in the kitchen as he opened the envelope. But this time all was not as usual. Papa caught his breath quickly, then read in a shaky voice: " 'Dear George, It seems to me such an impersonal thing just to mail you a check at Christmas, so I'm sending gifts this year which I hope you will all enjoy. Love, Robert.' "

Papa hid the dismay he must have been feeling. Mama couldn't help crying. Papa had a childlike faith in God to provide for his needs; oftener than not, God's provision was Mama. It was her worried-but-expert management that helped answer his prayers. Now even she was helpless.

The box with Uncle Robert's gifts arrived. We left it sealed and carried it into the parlor. For days we talked about what our gifts might be, and on Christmas morning we opened the box with unbridled hopes.

Alas, our hopes were quickly dashed! The expensive, handsome gifts each and all missed the mark. I was a tomboy and I craved a pair of bloomers—that daring garment introduced by the suffragettes. My gift was a doll. A sissy one. Pudgy young Rob, marbles champ of the fifth grade, got a telescope.

Papa had set his heart on new baptismal boots; his gift was a leisure jacket—and that was sad, because leisure was the one thing he had less of than money.

Mama's gift was a shocker. She wanted one of the new electric motors for her sewing machine so she wouldn't have to power it with her foot. Her gift was a big, gleaming, superelegant alligator handbag. Even I could see that she would look strange with a bag like the one the banker's wife carried to church.

When the last present had been opened we sat with the gifts in our laps and bright wrappings around us, too stunned to speak. Finally Papa rose to his feet.

"Fannie, children," he said gently, "I'm sure we each feel that Uncle Robert hasn't understood our needs and wishes this Christmas, that he's disappointed us. But I'm afraid we are the ones who don't understand. As we all know, my brother is a bachelor. He's not blessed as we are with Mother and with one another at Christmas each year. I'm sure he must feel lonely at such a time, but he's gone shopping for us this year, tried to imagine what he would want for Christmas if he were a merry ten-year-old like Grace or a middle-aged parson like me. He has given from the heart.

"If we find our gifts a little apart from our usual interests, we can also find that they open new doors." Leading the way, he slipped the brocaded jacket over his faded sweater. "My leisure coat will inspire me to take more time away from my busy schedule."

He suggested to us one by one how the gifts could bring a positive change to our lives. "Mildred's doll can lead her, we hope, to an interest in the domestic arts she'll need when her tree-climbing days are over. Rob's telescope can lift his eyes out of the playground sand for a look at the stars now and then."

And turning to Mama, "Fannie dear, I'm sure you'll find your magnificent bag a welcome touch of elegance in what I'm afraid is a pretty dreary wardrobe."

Each of us began to see our gifts and their giver with fresh vision. Love came into the room as an almost visible presence.

Mama began exploring the alligator bag and describing its wonders. "There's a green suede lining and a little amber comb. Even a secret pocket with a snap!" She reached in a finger and drew out a bit of paper. It was crisp, folded and green. It was the five hundred dollar check!

Then Papa's voice rose in rich cadence, firm as if he'd been fully expecting a miracle. "Praise God from whom all blessings flow!" And we all joined in.

It was the best of Christmases.

—*Mildred Morris*

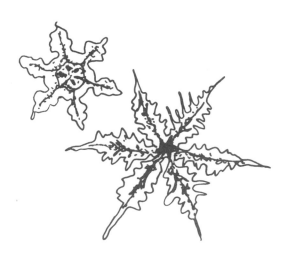

A Christmas List

"Ask," He said, "and you shall receive."
When you're nine years old, your heart can believe.
"Give me a doll that drinks and sleeps."
I asked, but oh, I didn't receive.

"Ask," He said, "and you shall receive."
I was young and in love, it was Christmas Eve.
"Give me the heart of that special boy."
I asked, but oh, I didn't receive.

"Ask," He said, "and you shall receive."
Money was scarce but I tried to believe.
"Give us enough for the gifts on our list."
I asked, but oh, I didn't receive.

"Ask," He said, "and you shall receive."
Sorting my values, I began to perceive.
"Give me Your Son. Let Him shine through me."
I asked, and lo, I began to receive . . .

More than I'd ever dared to believe
Treasures unmeasured, blessings undreamed,
All I'd asked or hoped to achieve.
"Ask," He said, "and you shall receive."

—*Marilyn Morgan Helleberg*

"Where Are Your Shoes?"

The people who report to us about the Quiet People they observe may be telling us about their own relatives—or it could be about utter strangers. In the "stranger" category is John Williams, who described an afternoon on the bus he drives in Milwaukee.

A week or so before Christmas, John was making his usual run westbound on Wisconsin Avenue. At the Marquette High School stop he picked up a bunch of boys who headed noisily for the back of the bus, horsing around, wisecracking. *Kids*, thought John Williams, shaking his head.

A few stops later, John pulled up in front of the Milwaukee County Medical Complex grounds, where a woman was waiting. She looked about thirty-five years old and her dingy gray coat was tattered from collar to hem. When she came up the steps of the bus, John saw she was wearing only socks on her feet.

"Where are your shoes?" John blurted.

"Is this bus going downtown?"

"Eventually we'll get downtown," John answered, still staring at her feet, "but right now we're going west."

"I don't mind the extra ride, as long as I can get warm." The woman paid her fare and sat down in a front seat.

John couldn't help himself. "Where are your shoes?" he asked again. "You can't be out on a day like today without shoes."

The woman sat up straighter in the seat and smoothed her coat. "Now, mister, don't you worry. The good Lord'll take care of me. Always has. I had enough to buy shoes for my kids and that's what counts."

John couldn't believe it. Here was a woman who didn't have any shoes on, telling *him* to stop worrying.

Before long, the bus pulled up at the 124th and Bluemound stop, where the high school crowd got off to transfer to another bus that would take them to their suburban homes. All the kids got off by the rear door—except one. This boy walked slowly up the aisle, then stopped in front of the woman and handed her his leather basketball shoes. "Here, lady, you take these." With that, he stepped off the bus and into the ten-degree chill in his stocking feet.

And that was how John Williams came to see the quietest of the Christmas quiet people in all of Milwaukee.

—The Editors

The Dream Horse _____

Do you remember the year, Dad, that you and I made our Christmas gift? I was only seven years old the afternoon I came running to you with news of my great discovery. Catching your hand, I pulled you into the field nearby and pushed back a tangle of honeysuckle. There, gazing up at us through glass eyes, was a discarded rocking horse, a once-proud wooden steed of grand style with a carved, curling mane and flowing tail. One of his legs was missing; the gilt of his bridle was chipped; the summer heat and rain had dulled his black enamel coat.

"Let's fix him!" you suggested, and carried him home on your shoulders.

The long November evenings were filled with our project. You did most of the work, of course, but I was at your side, helping, or, at least I thought I was helping. As you carved out a new leg to match its mates, we talked. We talked about Christmas and what it meant. We talked about what we were going to do with my horse when he was finished, and you were the first to mention families in which there are no daddies, and no toys.

At last the black enamel paint was dry, the bridle glistened with new gold, and my horse was well and strong again, his now sturdy legs stretching out into a swift gallop, his reins waiting for me to take hold. For several days I rode him ecstatically. On him, all dreams were real, all things possible—I could be a cowgirl, an Indian maiden, a princess. Together we rode into a world of adventure.

Too soon, though, the Salvation Army came to take my horse away—for I thought of him as mine now, despite the plans that you and I had made for him. I wept that day, Dad, as you know, for I felt the loss of him deeply.

But your wisdom shines through to me even now. The selfish seven-year-old girl in me surfaces more often than I would like to admit, and I know that giving is not always easy. But through the rocking horse, you showed me that giving has its own beautiful, not always obvious, rewards. Today, Dad, the thing I treasure most about "our" horse is not the glorious rides he gave me, or the happiness he brought to some unknown child; it's those long autumnal evenings you and I spent working and talking, together.

—*Rebekah Mikkelsen*

A Message from Mrs. Douse

I have a little story to tell, and I think it belongs here because it's a story of love in action, and that's what Christmas is all about.

In a midwestern city there is a company whose offices occupy a whole floor in a great skyscraper. In those offices, after each business day ended, worked an elderly, gray-haired woman. She worked into the late hours with brooms and mops.

It was a lonely, thankless job, but inside her glowed a remarkable and special kind of warmth: love for her bleak task; love for the great, impersonal city where she lived; love for her fellow human beings. And this love manifested itself in a most unusual way: Late at night, after her cleaning chores were done, she would sit in those empty offices and write little notes, full of concern and caring, to the daytime occupants.

An executive of the firm, a friend of mine, once showed me one of those notes. It went like this:

Dear Mr. Sales Manager:
    Your wastepaper baskets are very nice. Someone with a lot of imagination must have thought of making them. I like the picture of your family, too. What lovely children you have.

I am going home now. Most people are in bed, I suppose. It has been snowing and it is beautiful outside; the streets are so quiet. It will be lovely walking home tonight.

I just love to sit down and look at my work when it is well done. Even though I have to work so late, I'm glad that Jesus gives me strength to help out and to be happy doing it.

I must be going now. I promise not to write you again soon. It must be very boring.

Yours sincerely,
Mrs. Douse

That sales manager said to me, "How do you think a man feels when he gets a note like that? I can tell you: It does something to you. This woman, who has the love of Jesus Christ in her heart, just goes through an office building radiating it, loving people, loving the world, making it a more beautiful place. She comes in to clean the office, but she also cleans our minds and our souls. We have never seen her, but she has affected all of us."

Of course she affected them! She was able to do it because she had within her that steady flame of love, not just at Christmastime, but all through the year.

How can we find this spark within ourselves? How can we discover it, nurture it, make it grow? Our Christian faith tells us that there are many ways. By prayer, by church-going, by Bible reading. By practicing honesty and compassion in our daily lives. By being grateful for life and all the wonders it offers.

But most of all—once we have discovered it—by giving it away.

—*Norman Vincent Peale*

A Fair Share

I didn't think the Christmas spirit of giving was having much effect on my class of third graders. At our party all I heard was the usual chorus of "Gimme," "I want the biggest" and "Me first."

We'd been studying Mexican Christmas traditions and had made a *piñata*, a colorful papier-mâché animal that we'd filled with tiny presents and then dangled on a stout string. Following the Mexican custom, the blindfolded kids all took turns trying to crack the *piñata* open with a broomstick. When one youngster delivered the final blow, the children scrambled to the floor to pick up the loot. They hardly noticed Janine. As usual she stood to one side, much too timid to try for a prize.

There were several prizes left over, so I suggested we have a drawing for them. "Take a slip and write down the name of the boy or girl you think hasn't gotten a fair share," I said, hoping that somebody in the crowd would have noticed Janine.

I drew the first slip. "Janine," it said. She grinned and skipped up to receive her prize.

I drew the second slip, and the third and the fourth and the fifth. Here, at last, was the Christmas spirit I'd been missing. All the slips said the same thing: Janine.

—*Paula Stewart Marks*

The Secret of Happy Giving

Christmas—the time for giving and receiving gifts—is here again. Pondering the commercialism that seems to characterize this holiday season, I began to wonder if the Bible had anything to say about gifts and giving that might be helpful.

When I turned to it, one portion of the Sermon on the Mount seemed especially pertinent. If we stand in the temple, Jesus said, about to offer a gift to God, and suddenly remember that a friend has a grudge or resentment against us, we are to postpone giving the gift. We are to go and be reconciled to our friend, then come back and offer our gift to God; only then will He receive our offering and bless us. Relationships are primary, He seems to be saying; gifts secondary.

When the relationship *is* right, how precious the gift becomes. I remember the autumn my father spent many weeks making my Christmas gift—a doll bed, dresser and china cupboard. To this day I can shut my eyes and see that miniature furniture, painted white and with glass knobs on the drawers and cupboard doors. But surely the reason I remember it so fondly and in such detail is that the gift spoke of the father-daughter relationship behind it. The handmade furniture said, "I love you; you are important to me—important enough to be worth any amount of my time and my very best effort."

Such gifts are a spontaneous expression of unselfish love. But can we say the same for all the gifts that we give at Christmastime? Isn't it true that sometimes we use the device of a gift to conceal or paper over a flawed relationship? Or—even more common—isn't our attitude sometimes: "I'm giving you this gift because I feel I must (because you expect it, or because you're likely to give me something and I must reciprocate, or because I really don't know how to get out of this bleak and joyless exchange)"?

Perhaps this Christmas all of us should examine our gift lists to see if any of our giving falls into that category. If so, why not try the happy experiment of applying Jesus' priority to the situation: *First* be reconciled to thy brother, *then* offer thy gift.

We could try it with just one person. As we look down our list, is there anyone for whom we invariably have trouble finding a gift? Is there someone we resent shopping for? Anyone with whom we feel uncomfortable, no matter what we give them? Those can be clues to relationships that need mending.

Once we have selected the person, the next step is to devote time each day to thinking and praying about the relationship. Is the person a neighbor or a co-worker? Perhaps we've never really focused on him as a human being. We have not cared enough even to seek out his needs and preferences. The answer here could be a lunch date, a visit to his home, half an hour of real conversation. Does some old, never-acknowledged resentment lie between us and some member of the family? Healing could take the form of a letter, a face-to-face meeting or simply an interior act of confession.

Whatever the relationship we choose to work on and whatever the steps we take to improve it, we should wait until we are satisfied that it is as close to the one God intended as we can make it. Only then should we proceed with the secondary matter of selecting a gift. The price tag will not matter, as our gift does what all true gifts do—it reflects transparent love.

When we give in that spirit, we are truly making ready for Christmas when Love itself comes down to earth. Then with the Wise Men, we too can kneel at His crib and give thanks for the greatest gift of all.

—*Catherine Marshall*

Gift Exchange

In Sunday school at our Assembly of God church last year, it was announced that we'd be drawing names for a gift exchange. I groaned. *Another something to add to my too-long list!* But this exchange was different. We were asked to give a gift of prayer. For one month we were to pray for someone.

I knew the lady whose name I drew, but I didn't know what I should be praying for until I learned that she was unhappy because none of her family ever came to church with her. I prayed about that problem.

A month later, on the Monday after Christmas, we gathered at church to "exchange" our gifts. People told whom they had prayed for. We learned some amazing things. It was as if God Himself had selected the names for us.

Two men, whose friendship had become strained, unknowingly drew each other's names. As a result of their mutual prayers, they developed new understanding. Their closeness was restored.

And what happened to the woman *I* was praying for? I could hardly believe it when eleven members of her family came to church that day!

—*Edythe Nelson Crabb*

A Gift of the Heart _____

New York City, where I live, is impressive at any time, but as Christmas approaches it's overwhelming. Store windows blaze with lights and color, furs and jewels. Golden angels, forty feet tall, hover over Fifth Avenue. Wealth, power, opulence . . . nothing in the world can match this fabulous display.

Through the gleaming canyons, people hurry to find last-minute gifts. Money seems to be no problem. If there's a problem, it's that the recipients so often have everything they need or want that it's hard to find anything suitable, anything that will really say, "I love you."

One December, as Christ's birthday drew near, a stranger was faced with just that problem. She had come from Switzerland to live in an American home and perfect her English. In return, she was willing to act as secretary, mind the grandchildren, do anything she was asked. She was just a girl in her late teens. Her name was Ursula.

One of the tasks her employers gave Ursula was keeping track of Christmas presents as they arrived. There were many, and all would require acknowledgment. Ursula kept a faithful record, but with a growing sense of concern. She was grateful to her American friends; she wanted to show her gratitude by giving them a Christmas present. But nothing that she could buy with her small allowance could compare with the gifts she was recording daily. Besides, even without these gifts, it seemed to her that her employers already had everything.

At night from her window Ursula could see the snowy expanse of Central Park and beyond it the jagged skyline of the city. Far below, taxis hooted and the traffic lights winked red and green. It was so different from the silent majesty of the Alps that at times she had to blink back tears of the homesickness she was careful never to show. It was in the solitude of her little room, a few days before Christmas, that her secret idea came to Ursula.

It was almost as if a voice spoke clearly, inside her head. "It's true," said the voice, "that many people in this city have much more than you do. But surely there are many who have far less. If you will think about this, you may find a solution to what's troubling you."

Ursula thought long and hard. Finally on her day off, which was Christmas Eve, she went to a large department store. She moved slowly along the crowded aisles, selecting and rejecting things in her mind. At last she bought something and had it wrapped in gaily colored paper. She went out into the gray twilight and looked helplessly around. Finally, she went up to a doorman, resplendent in blue and gold. "Excuse, please," she said in her hesitant English, "can you tell me where to find a poor street?"

"A poor street, miss?" said the puzzled man.

"Yes, a very poor street. The poorest in the city."

The doorman looked doubtful. "Well, you might try Harlem. Or down in the Village. Or the Lower East Side, maybe."

But these names meant nothing to Ursula. She thanked the doorman and walked along, threading her way through the stream of shoppers until she came to a tall policeman. "Please," she said, "can you direct me to a very poor street in . . . in Harlem?"

The policeman looked at her sharply and shook his head. "Harlem's no place for you, miss." And he blew his whistle and sent the traffic swirling past.

Holding her package carefully, Ursula walked on, head bowed against the sharp wind. If a street looked poorer than the one she was on, she took it. But none seemed like the slums she had heard about. Once she stopped a woman, "Please, where do the very poor people live?" But the woman gave her a stare and hurried on.

Darkness came sifting from the sky. Ursula was cold and discouraged and afraid of becoming lost. She came to an intersection and stood forlornly on the corner. What she was trying to do suddenly seemed foolish, impulsive, absurd. Then, through the traffic's roar, she heard the cheerful tinkle of a bell. On the corner opposite, a Salvation Army man was making his traditional Christmas appeal.

At once Ursula felt better; the Salvation Army was a part of life in Switzerland too. Surely this man could tell her what she wanted to know. She waited for the light, then crossed over to him. "Can you help me? I'm looking for a baby. I have here a little present for the poorest baby I can find." And she held up the package with the green ribbon and the gaily colored paper.

Dressed in gloves and overcoat a size too big for him, he seemed a very ordinary man. But behind his steel-rimmed glasses his eyes were kind. He looked at Ursula and stopped ringing his bell. "What sort of present?" he asked.

"A little dress. For a small, poor baby. Do you know of one?"

"Oh, yes," he said. "Of more than one, I'm afraid."

"Is it far away? I could take a taxi, maybe?"

The Salvation Army man wrinkled his forehead. Finally he said, "It's almost six o'clock. My relief will show up then. If you want to wait, and if you can afford a dollar taxi ride, I'll take you to a family in my own neighborhood who needs just about everything."

"And they have a small baby?"

"A very small baby."

"Then," said Ursula joyfully, "I wait!"

The substitute bell-ringer came. A cruising taxi slowed. In its welcome warmth, Ursula told her new friend about herself, how she came to be in New York, what she was trying to do. He listened in silence, and the taxi driver listened too. When they reached their destination, the driver said, "Take your time, miss. I'll wait for you."

On the sidewalk, Ursula stared up at the forbidding tenement, dark, decaying, saturated with hopelessness. A gust of wind, iron-cold, stirred the refuse in the street and rattled the ashcans. "They live on the third floor," the Salvation Army man said. "Shall we go up?"

But Ursula shook her head. "They would try to thank me, and this is not from me." She pressed the package into his hand. "Take it up for me, please. Say it's from . . . from someone who has everything."

The taxi bore her swiftly back from dark streets to lighted ones, from misery to abundance. She tried to visualize the Salvation Army man climbing the stairs, the knock, the explanation, the package being opened, the dress on the baby. It was hard to do.

Arriving at the apartment house on Fifth Avenue where she lived, she fumbled in her purse. But the driver flicked the flag up. "No charge, miss."

"No charge?" echoed Ursula, bewildered.

"Don't worry," the driver said. "I've been paid." He smiled at her and drove away.

Ursula was up early the next day. She set the table with special care. By the time she had finished, the family was awake, and there was all the excitement and laughter of Christmas morning. Soon the living room was a sea of gay discarded wrappings. Ursula thanked everyone for the presents she received. Finally, when there was a lull, she began to explain hesitantly why there seemed to be none from her. She told about going to the department store. She told about the Salvation Army man. She told about the taxi driver. When she finished, there was a long silence. No one seemed to trust himself to speak. "So you see," said Ursula, "I try to do a kindness in your name. And this is my Christmas present to you . . ."

How do I happen to know all this? I know it because ours was the home where Ursula lived. Ours was the Christmas she shared. We were like many Americans, so richly blessed that to this child from across the sea there seemed to be nothing she could add to the material things we already had. And so she offered something of far greater value: a gift of the heart, an act of kindness carried out in our name.

Strange, isn't it? A shy Swiss girl, alone in a great impersonal city. You would think that nothing she could do would affect anyone. And yet, by trying to give away love, she brought the true spirit of Christmas into our lives, the spirit of selfless giving. That was Ursula's secret—and she shared it with us all.

—Norman Vincent Peale

The Lesson

It happened years ago on one of those raw December days that make people wish they had shopped in July. Snowflaked winds whipped through the streets. Hunched on a sidewalk bench sat an unshaven man. He wore a threadbare jacket and shoes with no socks. He had folded a paper bag around his neck to keep out the biting wind.

One shopper paused, saddened by the man. *Such a pity,* she thought. But there was really nothing she could do. While the shopper lingered, a little girl, eleven or twelve, walked by and spotted the frostbitten figure on the bench. Wrapped around the girl's neck was a bright red woolen scarf. She stopped beside the old man, unwrapped her red scarf and draped it tenderly about his neck. The child slipped away. The man rubbed the warm wool. And the shopper crept away, wishing she had been the one to give the scarf.

I was that shopper and God taught me something that day. Wherever I am, whatever I possess, there is always something I can give—a touch, a smile, a prayer, a kind word, even a red scarf.

—*Sue Monk Kidd*

A Gift for Antonio

He walked timidly up the front steps, an incredibly small, dirty, ragged child, shoeless and with a battered gray shoebox hanging by a worn leather strap from one shoulder. He seemed so small—hardly larger than my five-year-old—as he stretched to find the doorbell. I watched as my very large Honduran maid answered the door.

"*Si?*" she boomed impatiently.

"Zapatos?" (shoes) he whispered.

"No!" she answered.

Something about that little brown face peering up through the iron grillwork of my front porch and the huge stern face glowering down at him jarred my maternal instinct.

"Wait, Elena," I interrupted. "I do have some shoes he can polish."

Why this boy? I thought, as I selected some shoes to offer him. What had moved me about that tiny figure, so similar to the hundreds of other beggar children I'd seen at my door in the year since our family had come to live in Honduras? Why should the impersonal attitude I'd had to strive hard to achieve in order to survive emotionally in a poverty-filled country suddenly shatter at the sight of this one waif seeking work? That's it! He wasn't begging, though heaven knows he was every bit as shabbily attired as the others. He was asking for work—not a handout.

Try as I might, I couldn't help comparing him with Brian, our healthy, well-nourished youngster. The thought of my own little one in the horrible position of having to go out on the streets to earn a living was something my middle-class American upbringing wouldn't allow me to comprehend, let alone accept. It might be easy to picture Brian in a youthful game, with his father's shoeshine box under his arm, happily offering to polish my neighbor's shoes for a few pennies. But the idea of him pleading for work to earn enough for one meal a day—and maybe going hungry if he didn't succeed—was so repulsive to me that I quickly gathered up every shoe that even hinted it had been worn.

In the months that followed, Antonio became our regular weekly visitor. He worked diligently and long on each shoe, using his finger to spread the polish from minute rouge-sized cans. I'd never seen shoe polish sold in such a small container, and I realized Antonio must buy his supplies from his meager earnings.

Brian liked him and was more successful than the rest of us in getting him to relax a little and smile, though not even Brian could distract him until his job was finished.

Elena, whose stern countenance was an attempt to conceal a warm heart, always brought him a huge plate of rice, beans, tortillas and leftover meat. She would chat with him while he ate and thus learned that, though he was not much bigger than Brian, he was actually eleven years old, the eldest of five children, fatherless and with an invalid mother. He was the sole support of his entire family. I could hardly believe that this tiny child was only a year younger than our other son, Bruce, who looked much older and stronger.

When December came, the whole family, including Elena, discussed what gift we could give Antonio for Christmas. It shouldn't have been difficult—he had so little. But we wanted it to be something special—something he would like very much. Yet it was not an easy decision, since in all those months that he had worked for us, Antonio had never once asked for a thing from us except our business. We agreed to let Elena be our detective and try to uncover his innermost desires. Bruce and Brian were convinced that he must want toys or candy, but Elena reported that Antonio's dream was to have a new pair of long trousers.

"Shucks, that's nothing," said Bruce. "I have a whole drawer full of clothes that don't fit me any more." I tended to agree with him. Clothes had been on my list from the start, and we would give him some things Bruce had outgrown. But we wanted to give him something extra—something new.

Then Elena's native wisdom came through.

"*Señora,*" she offered, "don't give him something to play with. He's a very proud little man—*hombre.* Give him something he can use."

"I've got it, Mom!" cried Bruce. "Let's give him a new shoeshine kit. His is so old and ugly."

It was decided. Now we must plan it. It must be large enough to hold the larger, more economical cans of polish, plus brushes and buffers, which Antonio didn't then possess, and it must be brightly colored and cheerful. Elena knew of a carpenter who could make such a box for us.

That week was a joy. Every one of us was enthusiastically involved. When the carpenter presented the unpainted box, we could hardly wait to paint it and shop for the necessary items to go inside it. We chose a spray can of light green paint and the largest cans of polish in every color available. It was one of the happiest times I can remember—all the family together wholeheartedly trying to make someone else happy. Even Brian was able to do his share. After Bruce painted the box, Brian spent hours going through magazines for pictures of birds and flowers to cut out and glue on its sides. When it was all finished we stood around the table admiring it. There was no doubt in our minds that there was no finer shoebox anywhere.

"Mom, it's great!" said Bruce, frowning. "But what if somebody steals it?"

It made me proud to think that my spoiled, sometimes selfish twelve-year-old was concerned about a poor little Honduran boy's fate. Yet I knew his reasoning was sound. In a place where poverty abounds, the smaller child often falls prey to the older, bigger children. We had to devise a plan to protect Antonio.

In jet black paint we stenciled ANTONIO CRUZ across the front of the shoebox, and smugly agreed we'd done our best to thwart prospective thieves.

I don't know how we were able to keep our secret from the shoeshine boy until Christmas Eve, but we did. Early on the 24th, Bruce polished all the shoes in the house so there would be no work awaiting Antonio. When I offered him Antonio's usual fee, he put it neatly on top of the wrapped present under the tree. Brian jumped up and down when the doorbell rang. "Oh, I hope he likes it," he squealed.

Elena opened the door and invited Antonio inside. He stood very still, bewildered. Never before had he set foot inside our house. He always sat on the front steps to work. Elena prodded him into the living room where a mound of presents lay underneath our giant Christmas tree. Three grinning, excited Grahams were staring at him, and he didn't understand what was happening.

"Antonio," I said, "*San Nicolás* came early and left some gifts for you." I reached down and drew out our wrapped offerings. We had wrapped each item in a separate package, remembering that half the fun is in the opening.

He stood rigid, near the door, eyes wide, without smiling. If anything, his look registered fear, not joy.

"Open them! Open them!" shouted Brian as Antonio made no move to disturb the ribbons and paper. Prodded by us all, he opened the package of clothes slowly, carefully trying not to tear the paper; and just as carefully he rewrapped it. There was no change in his expression. I pushed the other small gifts at him, helping with the opening, and again noted nothing joyful in his eyes.

"This is the best of all," shouted Bruce, grabbing the shoebox and almost throwing it at Antonio. We were so keyed up that we must have seemed like maniacs to that small, quiet boy. We hovered over him as he painstakingly removed the wrappings on our treasure. Again there was nothing but nervousness emanating from Antonio.

"Say thank you, Antonio," interrupted Elena in her normal gruff manner.

"*Gracias,*" whispered the child, edging closer to the door.

Bruce looked at me, puzzled. I knew exactly what was bothering him because I felt the same disappointment. What had we done wrong?

Sensing that our little friend would continue to be miserable the longer we kept him on display, I helped him to gather his gifts together, put Bruce's money in his hand and opened the door so he could leave. Elena came bustling from the kitchen with his dinner—a double portion of everything—already wrapped in aluminum foil.

Antonio almost ran down the steps and into the street without a backward glance. He couldn't get away fast enough.

What can I tell the boys? I thought. *They tried so hard and gave so willingly.*

In the living room I put an arm around each silent, disappointed son. "Cheer up!" I began. "I'm sure Antonio liked your gifts. It's just that we were expecting him to get all excited, as we would have. Maybe he can't express his happiness in the same way we do. I know inside he was very pleased, but what is more important is that we all felt happy doing this for him."

Just then we caught a glimpse of Antonio through our huge circular window. He was sitting on the curb across the street. He had placed all his gifts on the sidewalk beside him. One by one he picked them up, stroking them, fondling them, savoring them. His face was bright with a joy I can't describe. The hot Honduran sun glistened as it shone on the tears running down his brown cheeks.

"*Feliz Navidad*—Merry Christmas, boys," I said, hugging them to me, "and to you, too, Antonio."

—Betty R. Graham

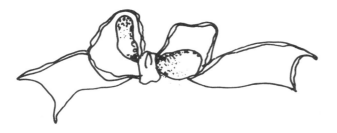

One Room, One Window ____

Mrs. Morton was an elderly widow and a permanent tenant in the guest house where I lived in Oakland, California.

Tony was, to us, simply a sullen man who owned the rooming house next door.

Once our house had been the mansion of a California senator; now it was a sheltering stronghold for teachers, business people and retirees. Many of the dwellings on once-fashionable Jackson Street, plush landmarks of an earlier era, had become victims of age. One such was the crumbling white house in which Tony and his wife lived.

Everyone on the block agreed that Tony was unfriendly, yet we had to admit that he worked untiringly in his garden and had restored his weed-rioting premises to prideful order. In that garden there was a huge magnolia tree, a beautiful tree which Tony worshiped much as the Druids did their oak. But one large branch shadowed our house and obscured the view from the single window of Mrs. Morton's room. Many times the old lady had wished aloud that the branch were not there. "I do believe I could see Lake Merritt," she would say wistfully. The lake was only a block distant.

Tactfully, Miss Plunkett, our housekeeper, suggested to Tony that he cut off the branch. He was outraged. Even I, one courage-giving, brisk October day, hinted to Tony how dark Mrs. Morton's room was. More outrage.

Then Christmas came. That morning I accompanied Miss Plunkett on her cheery rounds of the rooms and when we visited Mrs. Morton, we found her radiantly excited. "Come see!" she said, tugging us across the room.

Her window now framed a seascape of beauty; diamonds sparkled on the rippling blue waters of Lake Merritt. The obstructing branch had been cut away.

Miss Plunkett and I hastened next door to thank Tony. I think he was happy to see us, but he shuffled with embarrassment.

"How did you come to do it?" I asked.

Tony groped for expression. "It's Christmas," he said finally.

Christmas, I thought. The old wonderful miracle had repeated itself. Hearts are gentled. Strangers, however self-serving, bring gifts of brotherhood. . . .

"What a lovely gift," Miss Plunkett said.

"But, lady," he said, "*I got the gift.*"

We did not know what he meant until, beckoning us outside, Tony pointed, with surprised joy, to his cherished tree. "Look, she's more pretty than before!"

It was true. Removing the wayward limb had destroyed none of the tree's grace. Rather, the magnolia now towered heavenward with sharpened beauty, a symmetry that truly made it the showpiece of Tony's garden, quite the grandest "Christmas tree" on our block.

—Eva Dunbar

The More You Give

Give strength, give thought, give deeds, give wealth;
Give love, give tears, and give thyself.
Give, give, be always giving.
Who gives not is not living;
The more you give, the more you live.

—Author Unknown

The miracles of Christmas

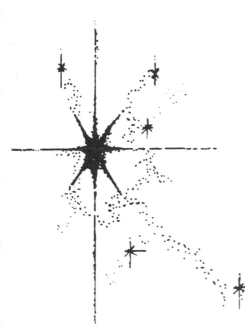

"The Miracle of Christmas"

The wonderment
        in a small child's eyes,
The ageless awe
        in the Christmas skies,
The nameless joy
        that fills the air,
The throngs that kneel
        in praise and prayer . . .
These are the things
        that make us know
That men may come
        and men may go,
But none will
        ever find a way
To banish Christ
        from Christmas Day . . .
For with each child
        there's born again
A *mystery* that baffles men.

—Helen Steiner Rice

Just One Small Candle

Queen Marie of Rumania loved to tell a story about a forest village in her country, and the poor people who lived there. Their poverty was most clearly reflected in the ramshackle church which stood near the town center. When visitors came, villagers often said apologetically, "Someday we're going to build a beautiful cathedral like the one on the other side of the forest."

Oh, how they did admire that neighboring church. In fact, on special occasions, they often trekked through the forest to the cathedral—it just seemed God was nearer to them in this majestic setting.

When they made the trip through the dense forest, however, it was necessary to pass by a well that was supposed to be haunted. It was said that if you didn't throw a coin into the well, something would drag you down into it and you would never be seen again.

One cold, dark Christmas Eve, a little boy named Raul passed by on his way to the cathedral, carrying only a small candle to light his path. Back in the village, Raul's widowed mother was dying. He hoped to place his candle on the altar and pray that she might be spared.

As he came near the well, he heard a moan. It was then he realized that he had forgotten to bring a coin. Terrified, Raul started to run. But he tripped on a root and fell by the well's edge. There he heard a child's voice, "Help me out! Give me your light so I can see my way."

"This candle is for my mother," Raul said, trembling. "I must take it to the altar of the big church so that she will get well."

"Can you refuse me on the night of Christ's birth?" the voice pleaded. The boy thought a moment. Then he threw the candle into the well and fell weeping on his knees in the darkness.

Suddenly, the light returned. Looking up, Raul saw a child stepping out of the well, holding the little candle in his hand. "Go back home," said the child. "Your mother will live."

Raul ran home and found his mother waiting for him as though she had never been ill. Later that night, they went together to the shabby village church to give thanks. When they entered they were nearly blinded by the light that streamed from the altar. Bathed in such splendor, the old church was every bit as beautiful as the neighboring cathedral.

"Why, Raul," exclaimed his mother, "there is only one candle on the altar. How can one candle make such light?"

Raul was too awed to speak, for as he knelt before the altar he saw that it was his very own candle. The light he had given away had been given back a thousandfold.

—*Norman Vincent Peale*

The Miraculous Staircase

On that cool December morning in 1878, sunlight lay like an amber rug across the dusty streets and adobe houses of Santa Fe. It glinted on the bright tile roof of the almost completed Chapel of Our Lady of Light and on the nearby windows of the convent school run by the Sisters of Loretto. Inside the convent, the Mother Superior looked up from her packing as a tap came on her door.

"It's *another* carpenter, Reverend Mother," said Sister Francis Louise, her round face apologetic. "I told him that you're leaving right away, that you haven't time to see him, but he says . . ."

"I know what he says," Mother Magdalene said, going on resolutely with her packing. "That he's heard about our problem with the new chapel. That he's the best carpenter in all of New Mexico. That he can build us a staircase to the choir loft despite the fact that the brilliant architect in Paris who drew the plans failed to leave any space for one. And despite the fact that five master carpenters have already tried and failed. You're quite right, Sister; I don't have time to listen to that story again."

"But he seems such a nice man," said Sister Francis Louise wistfully, "and he's out there with his burro, and . . ."

"I'm sure," said Mother Magdalene with a smile, "that he's a charming man, and that his burro is a charming donkey. But there's sickness down at the Santo Domingo Pueblo, and it may be cholera. Sister Mary Helen and I are the only ones here who've had cholera. So we have to go. And you have to stay and run the school. And that's that!" Then she called, "Manuela!"

A young Indian girl of twelve or thirteen, black-haired and smiling, came in quietly on moccasined feet. She was a mute. She could hear and understand, but the Sisters had been unable to teach her to speak. Mother Superior spoke to her gently: "Take my things down to the wagon, child. I'll be right there." And to Sister Francis Louise: "You'd better tell your carpenter friend to come back in two or three weeks. I'll see him then."

"Two or three weeks. Surely you'll be home for Christmas?"

"If it's the Lord's will, Sister. I hope so."

In the street, beyond the waiting wagon, Mother Magdalene could see the carpenter, a bearded man, strongly built and taller than most Mexicans, with dark eyes and a smiling, wind-burned face. Beside him, laden with tools and scraps of lumber, a small gray burro stood patiently. Manuela was stroking its nose, glancing shyly at its owner. "You'd better explain," said the Mother Superior, "that the child can hear him, but she can't speak."

Good-byes were quick—the best kind when you leave a place you love. Southwest, then, along the dusty trail, the mountains purple with shadow, the Rio Grande a ribbon of green far off to the right. The pace was slow, but Mother Magdalene and Sister Mary Helen amused themselves by singing songs and telling Christmas stories as the sun marched up and down the sky. And their leathery driver listened and nodded.

Two days of this brought them to Santo Domingo Pueblo, where the sickness was not cholera after all, but measles, almost as deadly in an Indian village. And so they stayed, helping the harassed Father Sebastian, visiting the dark adobe hovels where feverish brown children tossed and fierce Indian dogs showed their teeth.

At night they were bone-weary, but sometimes Mother Magdalene found time to talk to Father Sebastian about her plans for the dedication of the new chapel. It was to be in April; the Archbishop himself would be there. And it might have been dedicated sooner, were it not for this incredible business of a choir loft with no means of access—unless by ladder.

"I told the Bishop," said Mother Magdalene, "that it would be a mistake to have the plans drawn in Paris. If something went wrong, what could we do? But he wanted our chapel in Santa Fe patterned after the Sainte Chapelle in Paris, and who am I to argue with Bishop Lamy? So the talented Monsieur Mouly designs a beautiful choir loft high up under the rose window, and no way to get to it."

"Perhaps," sighed Father Sebastian, "he had in mind a heavenly choir. The kind with wings."

"It's not funny," said Mother Magdalene a bit sharply. "I've prayed and prayed, but apparently there's no solution at all. There just isn't room on the chapel floor for the supports such a staircase needs."

The days passed, and with each passing day Christmas drew closer. Twice, horsemen on their way from Santa Fe to Albuquerque brought letters from Sister Francis Louise. All was well at the convent, but Mother Magdalene frowned over certain paragraphs. "The children are getting ready for Christmas," Sister Francis Louise wrote in her first letter. "Our little Manuela and the carpenter have become great friends. It's amazing how much he seems to know about us all. . . ."

And what, thought Mother Magdalene, *is the carpenter still doing there?*

The second letter also mentioned the carpenter. "Early every morning he comes with another load of lumber, and every night he goes away. When we ask him by what authority he does these things, he smiles and says nothing. We have tried to pay him for his work, but he will accept no pay. . . ."

Work? What work? Mother Magdalene wrinkled up her nose in exasperation. Had that softhearted Sister Francis Louise given the man permission to putter around in the new chapel? With firm and disapproving hand, the Mother Superior wrote a note ordering an end to all such unauthorized activities. She gave it to an Indian pottery-maker on his way to Santa Fe.

But that night the first snow fell, so thick and heavy that the Indian turned back. Next day at noon the sun shone again on a world glittering with diamonds. But Mother Magdalene knew that another snowfall might make it impossible for her to be home for Christmas.

By now the sickness at Santo Domingo was subsiding. And so that afternoon they began the long ride back.

The snow did come again, making their slow progress even slower. It was late on Christmas Eve, close to midnight, when the tired horses plodded up to the convent door. But lamps still burned. Manuela flew down the steps, Sister Francis Louise close behind her. And chilled and weary though she was, Mother Magdalene sensed instantly an excitement, an electricity in the air that she could not understand.

Nor did she understand it when they led her, still in her heavy wraps, down the corridor, into the new, as-yet-unused chapel where a few candles burned. "Look, Reverend Mother," breathed Sister Francis Louise. "Look!"

Like a curl of smoke the staircase rose before them, as insubstantial as a dream. Its base was on the chapel floor; its top rested against the choir loft. Nothing else supported it; it seemed to float on air. There were no banisters. Two complete spirals it made, the polished wood gleaming softly in the candlelight. "Thirty-three steps," whispered Sister Francis Louise. "One for each year in the life of our Lord."

Mother Magdalene moved forward like a woman in a trance. She put her foot on the first step, then the second, then the third. There was not a tremor. She looked down, bewildered, at Manuela's ecstatic, upturned face. "But it's impossible! There wasn't time!"

"He finished yesterday," the Sister said. "He didn't come today. No one has seen him anywhere in Santa Fe. He's gone."

"But *who* was he? Don't you even know his *name*?"

The Sister shook her head, but now Manuela pushed forward, nodding emphatically. Her mouth opened; she took a deep, shuddering breath; she made a sound that was like a gasp in the stillness. The nuns stared at her, transfixed. She tried again. This time it was a syllable, followed by another. "Jo–se." She clutched the Mother Superior's arm and repeated the first word she had ever spoken. "Jose!"

Sister Francis Louise crossed herself. Mother Magdalene felt her heart contract. Jose—the Spanish word for Joseph. Joseph the Carpenter. Joseph the Master Woodworker of . . .

"Jose!" Manuela's dark eyes were full of tears. "Jose!"

Silence, then, in the shadowy chapel. No one moved. Far away across the snow-silvered town Mother Magdalene heard a bell tolling midnight. She came down the stairs and took Manuela's hand. She felt uplifted by a great surge of wonder and gratitude and compassion and love. And she knew what it was. It was the spirit of Christmas. And it was upon them all.

—*Arthur Gordon*

Author's note: The wonderful thing about legends is the way they grow. Through the years they can be told and retold and embroidered a bit more each time. This, indeed, is such a retelling. But all good legends contain a grain of truth, and in this case the irrefutable fact at the heart of the legend is the inexplicable staircase itself.

You may see it yourself in Santa Fe today. It stands just as it stood when the chapel was dedicated over ninety years ago—except for the banister, which was added later. Tourists stare and marvel. Architects shake their heads and murmur, "Impossible." No one knows the identity of the designer-builder. All the Sisters know is that the problem existed, a stranger came, solved it and left.

The thirty-three steps make two complete turns without central support. There are no nails in the staircase; only wooden pegs. The curved stringers are put together with exquisite precision; the wood is spliced in seven places on the inside and nine on the outside. The wood is said to be a hard-fir variety, nonexistent in New Mexico. School records show that no payment for the staircase was ever made.

Who is real and who is imaginary in this version of the story? Mother Mary Magdalene was indeed the first Mother Superior; she came to Santa Fe by riverboat and covered wagon in 1852. Bishop J. B. Lamy was indeed her Bishop. And Monsieur Projectus Mouly of Paris was indeed the absentminded architect.

Sister Francis Louise? Well, there must have been someone like her. And Manuela, the Indian girl, came out of nowhere to help with the embroidery.

The carpenter himself? Ah, who can say?

The Christmas That _____
Changed a Town's Name

River Fork was a small town, a friendly town, except for the Fletchers and the McCloskeys. They hadn't spoken to each other for two generations. No one seemed to know why they hated each other, not even the Fletchers and the McCloskeys. But the Fletchers did not speak to the McCloskeys and the McCloskeys did not speak to the Fletchers.

One night shortly before one Christmas something happened to change that and anyone who was there will tell you what made the citizens of River Fork also change their town's name.

It all began one November morning when plump, motherly Mrs. Parris happily made an announcement to her fifth grade class: "This coming Christmas, children, our class has been selected to give a Christmas Play! We will begin choosing those who will play various parts and everyone will have *some* part in the play." Upon hearing this, the children clapped and squealed.

And so the players were selected and each child who had a speaking part was given a simple script.

The sixth graders were given the job of making the stage scenery. The seventh graders would play the music and parents would, as usual, be asked to make the costumes and provide refreshments. Mrs. Parris was determined to make this the best Christmas play the school had ever put on.

The list went on . . . Mr. Loveliss had agreed to lend a small, gentle burro and Mr. Baker promised to provide straw for the stable from his grain and feed store. One thing bothered Mrs. Parris, however—the infant Jesus. In almost all Nativity plays, a doll was used in the manger. But Mrs. Parris wanted it to be really special . . . the infant should be a real child. But who would lend a new baby for the school play? She decided to ask her students what *they* thought. She'd learned long ago that children were smarter than grown-ups believed they were—especially if given the opportunity to express themselves.

She asked her class what *they* thought of her idea of a live baby for the play, and the children all agreed—they wanted a real baby to be in the manger. That settled it. So next she asked if anyone had a baby brother. Only one hand was raised. It was Amanda Fletcher. "Yes, Amanda? Do *you* have a small baby brother?"

"No, ma'am, but I have a baby sister. She's three months old and she never cries."

Aaron McCloskey snorted. "Jesus wasn't a girl. That's dumb. A girl for the Baby Jesus!"

"Now wait a moment, children," said Mrs. Parris. "The baby will be in a manger, so no one will *know* if it's a boy or girl. I shall call your mother tonight, Amanda."

That night Mrs. Parris phoned Mrs. Fletcher who listened, then said: "Amanda already told me of the Christmas play. She's delighted she was chosen to play the part of Mary and more delighted that you want Christina to be the Infant Jesus."

"*Christina*—oh, how beautiful! And so appropriate," said Mrs. Parris.

Mrs. Fletcher sighed. "There is something we haven't told Amanda yet. We took Christina to the doctor last week . . ." Her voice broke slightly. "The doctor says Christina has no voice. She cannot cry, nor will she ever be able to speak."

Mrs. Parris was stunned. "I'm *so* sorry."

"I thought you should know. But if you still want Christina in the play, I shall bring her. With Amanda so near, I'm sure the baby won't be upset."

On the night of the play, little Christina lay in the manger, squirming and kicking her feet for all to see. She actually seemed to enjoy the attention.

At the climax of the play, the stage lights dimmed except for one spotlight focused on the manger. The figures of Joseph, Mary and the Wise Men knelt in prayer. Offstage, the chorus began to sing, "It came upon the midnight clear . . ." And as they sang, the baby's arms waved.

As the last notes of the old song died away, Aaron McCloskey, dressed as an angel wearing dark horn-rimmed glasses, came out on stage. A blue spotlight held him in its light. He spread his arms wide and in a loud, high-pitched voice recited flatly, "May the Holy Birth bring joy into the hearts of each and every one of us this Christmas!"

He was supposed to leave the stage at this point, but instead, all the thoughts that had long been buried inside the boy came rushing out. In a voice that was now filled with genuine emotion he added:

"And may my parents and Amanda's parents be friends again!" He turned and ran from the stage.

There was stunned silence in the auditorium. From the rear of the auditorium someone said "Amen," and the applause began. Then, as if in agreement, a small cry came from the manger and a tiny arm waved vigorously.

Mrs. Fletcher leaped to her feet and raced onto the stage. She picked up the wailing Christina and held her up for all to see. "Praise God," she shouted, "it's a miracle!"

Word spread quickly about the miracle, for no one had known about Christina's condition. The following Sunday, everyone in River Fork was in church. The Fletchers and McCloskeys shared the same pew and Amanda hoped Christina wouldn't disturb the service.

Reverend Adams stepped to the pulpit. "Friends, I'm not going to try to understand or explain what happened in the school auditorium last night. But we sure saw a couple of miracles happen." He stared directly at the McCloskeys and Fletchers.

"I want to propose that we do something to remind us all of this great wonder. I propose we change the name of our town from River Fork to—Miracle."

The shouts and applause were enough to convince everyone it was a good idea.

Once again a baby had reached into the hearts of people and left the priceless gift of love. And to this day it's said you'll never find a town where there's more love than in the town of Miracle.

—*Martin Buxbaum*

Undelivered Gifts ⸺

Have you ever had the experience of *almost not doing* an act of thoughtfulness or charity—only to discover later that without this action on your part a very important experience would not have happened to someone else?

Whenever I am tempted to be lazy or indifferent in this way, I inevitably think back to that Christmas in Korea, in 1951.

It was late afternoon on December 24. After a cold, miserable ride by truck in the snow, I was back at our Command Post. Shedding wet clothing, I relaxed on a cot and dozed off. A young soldier came in and in my sleep-fogged condition I heard him say to the clerk, "I wish I could talk to the Sergeant about this."

"Go ahead," I mumbled, "I'm not asleep."

The soldier then told me about a group of Korean civilians four miles to the north who had been forced to leave their burning village. The group included one woman ready to give birth. His information had come from a Korean boy who said these people badly needed help.

My first inner reaction was: How could we ever find the refugees in this snow? Besides, I was dead tired. Yet something told me we should try.

"Go get Crall, Pringle and Graff," I said to the clerk. When these soldiers arrived I told them my plan, and they agreed to accompany me. We gathered together some food and blankets. Then I saw the box of Christmas packages in the corner of the office. They were presents sent over from charity organizations in the States. We collected an armful of packages and started out by jeep.

After driving several miles, the snow became so blinding that we decided to approach the village by foot. After what seemed like hours, we came to an abandoned Mission.

The roof was gone, but the walls were intact. We built a fire in the fireplace, wondering what to do next. Graff opened one of the Christmas packages in which he found some small, artificial Christmas trees and candles. These he placed on the mantel of the fireplace.

I knew it made no sense to go on in this blizzard. We finally decided to leave the food, blankets and presents there in the Mission in the hope that some needy people would find them. Then we groped our way back to the Command Post.

In April 1952, I was wounded in action and taken to the hospital at Won Ju. One afternoon while basking in the sun, a Korean boy joined me. He was a talkative lad and I only half listened as he rambled on.

Then he began to tell me a story that literally made me jump from my chair. After he finished, I took the boy to our chaplain; he helped me find an elder of the local Korean church who verified the boy's story.

"Yes, it was a true miracle—an act of God," the Korean churchman said. Then he told how on the previous Christmas Eve he was one of a group of Korean civilians who had been wandering about the countryside for days after North Korean soldiers had burned their village. They were nearly starved when they arrived at an old Mission. A pregnant woman in their group was in desperate condition.

"As we approached the Mission, we saw smoke coming from the chimney," the Korean said. "We feared that North Korean soldiers were there, but decided to go in anyway. To our relief, the Mission was empty. But, lo and behold, there were candles on the mantel, along with little trees! There were blankets and boxes of food and presents! It was a miracle!"

The old man's eyes filled with tears as he described how they all got down on their knees and thanked God for their deliverance. They made a bed for the pregnant woman and built a little shelter over her. There was plenty of wood to burn and food to eat and they were comfortable for the first time in weeks. It was Christmas Eve.

"The baby was born on Christmas Day," the man said. He paused. "The situation couldn't have been too different from that other Birth years ago."

On the following morning American soldiers rescued the Koreans, who later became the nucleus of a Christian church in the village where I was recuperating.

You just never know when you have a special role to play in one of God's miracles.

—*Wayne Montgomery*

Surprise Ending _____

I turned up the fur collar of my coat against a near-freezing wind as I stepped from our warm station wagon into the bare dirt of a front yard on the outskirts of town. Our adult Sunday school class had chosen the address from a Salvation Army list in the evening paper and my husband and I had driven out to meet the family. The idea was to find out their immediate needs so that we could provide a merry Christmas for them, and then, more important, to work with them throughout the year to try to make a real difference, a Christian difference, in their lives.

We had asked God to guide us to the right family, but now it looked as though the house we had chosen was going to be empty. No smoke came from the chimney and in the front door there was only a hole where a knob and a lock might have been, once. But when we knocked, the rag of curtain at the window moved and a small face peered out. A minute passed and then the door was opened by a boy about eight years old.

"Hello," I said. "Is your mother home?"

"Mama not home," he announced gravely. "She workin'."

"Well, ah—is any grownup here with you?" He shook his head.

"Let's step in for a minute," my husband suggested. "The house'll get cold with the door standing open." The boy moved shyly back and we entered the tiny room.

I'll never forget what we saw. There was a bed, sagging to the floor, the mattress oozing stuffing at every rip and seam. No sheets, no blankets. A small chest of drawers in the corner held a dusty glass punch bowl with cups hanging around the rim. A Bible lay beside it. On the floor a chipped enamel pan held some lumps of corn meal mush the children had been eating by fistfuls. The black wood stove was icy cold.

The boy who had let us in now stood protectively between two smaller children, a boy and a girl. Her oversized slacks were held together by a safety pin. All three youngsters were barefoot.

And there was a baby. He was lying on a pile of straw and rags that had once been an upholstered chair. He was wearing a remnant of an undershirt and a diaper that hadn't been changed for a long time.

I thought of my own warmly dressed children and baby in her

lovely birch crib with its clean white sheets and started to cry. I'd never really seen poverty before.

That afternoon we went back with blankets, diapers, food and clothes. Again, the mother was not home. But apparently she'd been home long enough to build a roaring fire, so hot the children had the front door standing wide open. A coal scuttle held scraps of linoleum from a pile of debris in the yard next door.

The next day we finally found the mother at home. Her name was Virginia and the children, in order of age, were Arthur Lee, Violet, Danny and the baby, David Ray. Virginia was a tiny woman in a yellow bouffant-organdy dress. She answered our questions quietly and was not offended that we had come to help.

What did she need most? A refrigerator so the baby's milk wouldn't sour, and something for the stove that wouldn't burn as fast as linoleum . . .

The class found a refrigerator, a bed, a crib, several chairs, sheets, more blankets. On Christmas, there were toys for the children and clothes and food for everyone. The wood stove was replaced by an oil heater that would not go out while the mother was away. The class pledged the money to pay the oil bills for the coming year.

The family's immediate physical needs had been relatively easy to satisfy. But what about the Christian difference?

Every week or two my husband and I would go to see Virginia and her family. Sometimes we'd carry hand-me-downs, or groceries, or books, sometimes we'd go empty-handed, just to visit. But she always gave us the same warm greeting. I remember the pride with which she invited me to sit down. She hadn't been able to exercise that kind of courtesy before, when she had no chairs.

Frequently, our four older children went along with us on these visits, and occasionally we took the baby. I had to explain to Virginia about our baby. German measles during my pregnancy had left little Marguerite deaf. When I told Virginia that the doctors said nothing could be done about it, I could see she was deeply affected.

On our next visit she greeted us with shining eyes. "Oh, Mrs. Harrell," she said, "I believe God is going to make your baby hear! Don't you feel it too? Can't she already hear a lot better than she could? I've been praying so hard ever since you told me. I *know* she's going to hear!"

I just smiled at Virginia. She didn't know as much about science as I did. I couldn't expect her to understand that nerve deafness was not curable. Of course *I* had prayed for my child; but my prayers had been ones of thankfulness for her, not prayers for healing. I took the doctors' words as final.

Marguerite was almost a year old when we first noticed the change in her. For a while we couldn't believe it ourselves, but at last we became convinced that she really was hearing certain loud sounds. When we took her back to the hearing clinic for testing, there was no doubt about it. Our daughter, whose nerve deafness had been pronounced complete and incurable, had begun to hear! In four short months her diagnosis had changed from "profoundly deaf" to "moderately to severely hard of hearing."

The doctors were amazed, but Virginia wasn't even surprised. "God did it, Mrs. Harrell. Didn't I ask Him for an icebox and a good stove, and didn't He give them to me? There's nothing He can't do, if we just ask Him."

I stared at her, trying to understand faith like this, reaching out my own feeble portion to try to take hold of hers.

"Mrs. Harrell," she said, "I'm going to keep on praying for that baby."

"Yes!" I whispered, "please keep praying. Don't ever stop."

It worked, you see, our Christmas project; it even accomplished the "Christian difference." Of course, the difference was in our lives, not Virginia's. But then, we'd asked God to guide us to the poor, and He generally knows where they are.

—*Irene B. Harrell*

An Exchange of Gifts

I grew up believing that Christmas was a time when strange and wonderful things happened, when wise and royal visitors came riding, when at midnight the barnyard animals talked to one another, and in the light of a fabulous star God came down to us as a little Child. Christmas to me has always been a time of enchantment, and never more so than the year that my son Marty was eight.

That was the year that my children and I moved into a cozy trailer home in a forested area just outside of Redmond, Washington. As the holiday approached, our spirits were light, not to be dampened even by the winter rains that swept down Puget Sound to douse our home and make our floors muddy.

Throughout that December Marty had been the most spirited, and busiest, of us all. He was my youngest, a cheerful boy, blond-haired and playful, with a quaint habit of looking up at you and cocking his head like a puppy when you talked to him. Actually the reason for this was that Marty was deaf in his left ear, but it was a condition that he never complained about.

For weeks I'd been watching Marty. I knew that something was going on with him that he was not telling me about. I saw how *eagerly* he made his bed, took out the trash, and *carefully* set the table and helped Rick and Pam prepare dinner before I got home from work. I saw how he silently collected his tiny allowance and tucked it away, spending not a cent of it. I had no idea what all this quiet activity was about, but I suspected that somehow it had something to do with Kenny.

Kenny was Marty's friend, and ever since they'd found each other in the springtime, they were seldom apart. If you called to one, you got them both. Their world was in the meadow, a horse pasture broken by a small winding stream, where the boys caught frogs and snakes, where they'd search for arrowheads or hidden treasure, or where they'd spend an afternoon feeding peanuts to the squirrels.

Times were hard for our little family, and we had to do some scrimping to get by. With my job as a meat wrapper and with a lot of ingenuity around the trailer, we managed to have elegance on a shoestring. But not Kenny's family. They were desperately poor, and his mother was having a real struggle to feed and clothe her two children. They were a good, solid family; but Kenny's mom was a proud woman, very proud, and she had strict rules.

How we worked, as we did each year, to make our home festive for the holiday! Ours was a handcrafted Christmas of gifts hidden away and ornaments strung about the place.

Marty and Kenny would sometimes sit still at the table long enough to help make cornucopias or weave little baskets for the tree;

but then, in a flash, one would whisper to the other, and they would be out the door and sliding cautiously under the electric fence into the horse pasture that separated our home from Kenny's.

One night shortly before Christmas, when my hands were deep in *peppernöder* dough, shaping tiny nutlike Danish cookies heavily spiced with cinnamon, Marty came to me and said in a tone mixed with pleasure and pride, "Mom, I've bought Kenny a Christmas present. Want to see it?" *So that's what he's been up to,* I said to myself. "It's something he's wanted for a long, long time, Mom."

After carefully wiping his hands on a dish towel, he pulled from his pocket a small box. Lifting the lid, I gazed at the pocket compass that my son had been saving all those allowances to buy. A little compass to point an eight-year-old adventurer through the woods.

"It's a lovely gift, Martin," I said, but even as I spoke, a disturbing thought came to mind. I knew how Kenny's mother felt about their poverty. They could barely afford to exchange gifts among themselves, and giving presents to others was out of the question. I was sure that Kenny's proud mother would not permit her son to receive something he could not return in kind.

Gently, carefully, I talked over the problem with Marty. He understood what I was saying.

"I know, Mom, I *know* . . . but what if it was a *secret?* What if they never found out *who* gave it?"

I didn't know how to answer him. I just didn't know.

The day before Christmas was rainy and cold and gray. The three kids and I all but fell over one another as we elbowed our way about our little home, putting finishing touches on Christmas secrets and preparing for family and friends who would be dropping by.

Night settled in. The rain continued. I looked out the window over the sink and felt an odd sadness. How mundane the rain seemed for a Christmas Eve. Would wise and royal men come riding on such a night? I doubted it. It seemed to me that strange and wonderful things happened only on clear nights, nights when one could at least see a star in the heavens.

I turned from the window, and as I checked on the ham and *lefse* bread warming in the oven, I saw Marty slip out the door. He wore his coat over his pajamas, and he clutched a tiny, colorfully wrapped box in his pocket.

Down through the soggy pasture he went, then a quick slide under the electric fence and across the yard to Kenny's house. Up the steps on tiptoes, shoes squishing; open the screen door just a crack; the gift placed on the doorstep; then a deep breath, a reach for the doorbell and a press on it *hard.*

Quickly Marty turned, ran down the steps and across the yard in a wild race to get away unnoticed. Then, suddenly, he banged into the electric fence.

The shock sent him reeling. He lay stunned on the wet ground. His body tingled and he gasped for breath. Then slowly, weakly, confused and frightened, he began the grueling trip back home.

"Marty," we cried as he stumbled through the door, "what happened?" His lower lip quivered, his eyes brimmed.

"I forgot about the fence, and it knocked me down!"

I hugged his muddy little body to me. He was still dazed, and there was a red mark beginning to blister on his face from his mouth to his ear. Quickly I treated the blister and, with a warm cup of cocoa soothing him, Marty's bright spirits returned. I tucked him into bed and just before he fell asleep he looked up at me and said, "Mom, Kenny didn't see me. I'm sure he didn't see me."

That Christmas Eve I went to bed unhappy and puzzled. It seemed such a cruel thing to happen to a little boy while on the purest kind of Christmas mission, doing what the Lord wants us all to do, giving to others, and giving in secret at that. I did not sleep well that night. Somewhere deep inside I think I must have been feeling the disappointment that the night of Christmas had come and it had been just an ordinary, problem-filled night, no mysterious enchantment at all.

But I was wrong.

By morning the rain had stopped and the sun shone. The streak on Marty's face was very red, but I could tell that the burn was not serious. We opened our presents, and soon, not unexpectedly, Kenny was knocking on the door, eager to show Marty his new compass and tell about the mystery of its arrival. It was plain that Kenny didn't suspect Marty at all, and while the two of them talked, Marty just smiled and smiled.

Then I noticed that while the two boys were comparing their Christmases, nodding and gesturing and chattering away, Marty was not cocking his head. When Kenny was talking, Marty seemed to be listening with his deaf ear. Weeks later a report came from the school nurse, verifying what Marty and I already knew: "Marty now has complete hearing in *both* ears."

The mystery of how Marty regained his hearing, and still has it, remains just that—a mystery. Doctors suspect, of course, that the shock from the electric fence was somehow responsible. Perhaps so. Whatever the reason, I just remain thankful to God for the good exchange of gifts that was made that night.

So you see, strange and wonderful things still happen on the night of our Lord's birth. And one does not have to have a clear night, either, to follow a fabulous star.

—Diane Rayner

That Holy Thing

They all were looking for a king
   To slay their foes and lift them high;
Thou cam'st, a little baby thing
   That made a woman cry.

O Son of Man, to right my lot
   Naught but thy presence can avail;
Yet on the road thy wheels are not,
   Nor on the sea thy sail!

My how or why thou wilt not heed,
   But come down thine own secret stair,
That thou mayst answer all my need—
   Yea, every bygone prayer.

—George MacDonald

Epilogue:
a lasting
Christmas

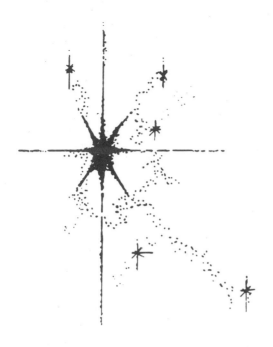

A Lasting Christmas

I keep a part of Christmas,
For it helps to add a glow
To the January darkness
And the February snow.
If March is cold and blustery,
And though April brings us rain,
The peace and warmth of Christmas
With its happiness remain . . .

There's a beauty when it's Christmas,
All the world is different then,
There's no place for petty hatred
In the hearts and minds of men.
That is why my heart is happy
And my mind can hold a dream,
For I keep a part of Christmas
With its peace and joy supreme.

—*Garnett Ann Schultz*

After-Christmas Presents

It is June. Outside the flowers are blooming, the sun is shining, and I am enjoying a Christmas present.

Last summer, Danny, the little boy from down the street, asked if he could mow my lawn for two dollars.

Poor little guy, I thought, *probably trying to earn a little money.* He would have no way of knowing how small a retired teacher's check could be in these days of inflation.

My yard is small. I could mow it myself. And two dollars was more than I could really afford. I had to turn him down.

Then came fall and the winter snow, and the lawn was forgotten.

Christmas Eve I was hanging a wreath on my door when Danny came again.

"Well, now," I said, smiling at him, "I do not believe the lawn needs mowing today."

"I brought you a Christmas present," he said, handing me an envelope. Then looking a little embarrassed he quickly said good-bye.

I opened the letter and I shall never forget the contents, written in a childish hand.

Dear neighbor:
I have a present for you. Next summer I will mow your lawn
all summer. Merry Christmas.

Danny

Danny has done far more than mow my lawn this summer. He has taught me that the gift worth giving is the gift of self. This Christmas I will have gifts for *my* neighbors, little favors that I can do for them throughout the year.

I hope, like me, they will all be enjoying my Christmas gifts when flowers are blooming and the sun is shining.

—Laura Norman

Christmas Every Day _____

Last year, as December 25th drew nearer and our mail box grew fuller, our family would tear open envelope after envelope of Christmas greetings; we'd read each card hastily, express delight and gratitude over hearing from this friend and that, and then each card would be added to the pile. On Christmas Day we just happened to make a count of the cards we had received. There were 365 of them.

"One for every day of the year," one of us remarked.

That was the beginning of a daily ritual in our home. We placed all the cards in a box in the dining room and every evening one card was selected for reading at the dinner table. The messages of beauty and love and inspiration, all too nearly submerged at Christmastime, now had new meaning; and now we had time to pray a special prayer for the friend who had sent the card.

This has been in reality the "year of the Lord" and has illustrated the truth, "For unto you is born this day . . . a Saviour, which is Christ the Lord."* Our home has become a Bethlehem—which in Hebrew means "house of bread"—as we pore over our cards and partake each night of God's Immortal Bread.

—*Edward A. Puff*

Christmas Is Always _____

Christmas was not just a starlit night in Bethlehem: it had been behind the stars forever.

There was Christmas in the heart of God when He made the earth, and then gave it away—to us. When He sent us His prophets, that was Christmas too. And it was the most magnificent Christmas of all, that night in Bethlehem when He gave us His own son.

*Luke 2:11.

As Jesus grew up, Christmas was everywhere He went, giving food, giving sight, giving life. For Christmas is giving.

But Christmas is also receiving. In the Bible it says: "As many as received him, to them gave he power to become the sons of God. . . ."*

As many as received Him! When we understand that, we understand that receiving can be even more important than giving—at Christmas! When we receive Christ, we experience completely the gift that is Christmas.

Then, for us, Christmas is truly always, for Jesus said, "Lo, I am with you always. . . ."**

And Christmas is Jesus!

—Dale Evans Rogers

The Afterglow

The greetings and carols have ended,
The glad celebrations have ceased
With the angels ascended to heaven,
The Wise Men returned to the East.
But the light that once shone on a manger
Still brightens the world from afar,
And listening hearts still hear angels,
And wise men still follow a star.

—Ellis Rowsey

*John 1:12   **Matthew 28:20